THE TAROT COMPANION

**THIS BOOK IS DEDICATED TO ALL STUDENTS OF TAROT.
MAY YOUR UNIQUE JOURNEY THROUGH THE CARDS BRING
YOU GREAT REWARDS.**

Brimming with creative inspiration, how-to projects, and useful information to enrich your everyday life, Quarto Knows is a favorite destination for those pursuing their interests and passions. Visit our site and dig deeper with our books into your area of interest: Quarto Creates, Quarto Cooks, Quarto Homes, Quarto Lives, Quarto Drives, Quarto Explores, Quarto Gifts, or Quarto Kids.

© 2018 Quarto Publishing Group USA Inc.
Text © 2015 Fair Winds Press

First Published in 2018 by Fair Winds Press, an imprint of The Quarto Group,
100 Cummings Center, Suite 265-D, Beverly, MA 01915, USA.
T (978) 282-9590 F (978) 283-2742 QuartoKnows.com

Fair Winds Press titles are also available at discount for retail, wholesale, promotional, and bulk purchase. For details, contact the Special Sales Manager by email at specialsales@quarto.com or by mail at The Quarto Group, Attn: Special Sales Manager, 100 Cummings Center, Suite 265-D, Beverly, MA 01915, USA.

Illustrations from the Rider-Waite Tarot Deck® reproduced by permission of U.S. Games Systems, Inc., Stamford, CT 06902 USA. Copyright © 1971 by U.S. Games Systems, Inc. Further reproduction prohibited. The Rider-Waite Tarot Deck® is a registered trademark of U.S. Games Systems, Inc.

The content for this book originally appeared in *The Ultimate Guide to Tarot* (Fair Winds Press, 2015) by Liz Dean.

22 21   11

ISBN: 978-1-59233-821-4

Digital edition published in 2018

Design, cover image, and page layout: The Lost & Found Dept.

Printed in China

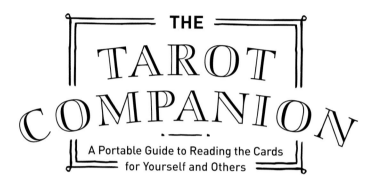

THE TAROT COMPANION

A Portable Guide to Reading the Cards for Yourself and Others

LIZ DEAN
author of *The Art of Tarot* and *The Golden Tarot*

FAIR WINDS

CONTENTS

INTRODUCING THE TAROT

Tarot is a system of archetypes, a picture-book of the human condition, reflecting our states of mind and stages of life. Over the past six hundred years, people have consulted the cards for religious instruction, spiritual insight, self-knowledge, and divining the future. The ancient symbols we see on the cards are designed to stimulate our intuition, connecting us with our higher selves or our divine or spiritual aspect.

REGULAR TAROT PRACTICE HAS MANY PERSONAL BENEFITS, INCLUDING:

INCREASED SELF-AWARENESS: Tarot gives you space to focus on yourself.

ENHANCED CREATIVITY: A tarot reading can offer a different perspective on a problem and innovative ways forward.

BETTER-HONED INTUITION AND PSYCHIC ABILITY: Tarot helps you see probable future events and influences.

A WAY TO EMPOWER OTHERS TO FIND THEIR SPIRITUAL PATH.

Anyone can learn to work with tarot and can benefit greatly from its insights; all you need is an open mind and a willingness to trust the impressions you sense during a reading.

A NOTE ON THE RIDER-WAITE TAROT

Myriad versions and styles of tarot decks have been created through the years. The tarot deck shown throughout this book is the Universal Waite, an enhanced Rider-Waite deck. The original Rider-Waite was devised by A. E. Waite and published by Rider, London. It is considered the most influential contemporary deck and has inspired many variants. The deck should properly be known as the Rider-Waite Smith, to honor the illustrator, Pamela Colman Smith.

HOW TO BEGIN

Tarot cards, like people, draw in energy. It's important not to let others touch your cards casually; they hold your energies and intentions, and are personal to you. Here are ways to attune to your new deck, cleanse the cards before a reading session, and protect them when you are not using them.

ATTUNING TO A NEW DECK

The process of connecting with your cards is called attuning. The more connected you feel to your cards, the more accurate, insightful, and inspiring your readings can be.

Before you begin reading a new deck of tarot cards, attune to them for exactly seven days by sleeping with your cards under your pillow. Look at the cards daily and touch them so your energy becomes imprinted upon them. Some readers attune to their cards through visualization. Try this:

1. Hold your cards in your right hand.
2. Close your eyes, take a deep breath, and visualize light pouring down through the crown of your head, third-eye chakra, throat, and heart, then down your right arm, into your right hand, and into the cards.
3. Imagine your cards filling with pure light. If you work with spirit guides or angels, ask them to come close and to help and protect you during the reading.
4. Open your eyes when you are ready.

CLEANSING YOUR DECK BEFORE A READING SESSION

When you take out your cards, clear away any old energy as follows:

1. Hold the cards in one hand and fan them out.
2. Gently blow on the card edges. You can do this in one breath.
3. Put the cards back in a neat pile, still holding them in one hand, and then knock firmly once on the top of the deck. It is ready to use.

PROTECTING YOUR CARDS WHEN YOU'RE NOT USING THEM

Your cards hold your energy imprint. Cards may pick up extraneous or negative energy from people and spaces, which can affect your readings. So when you are not using your cards, protect them from the environment, both physically and energetically. Keep them wrapped in a cloth of a dark color, such as deep purple cotton or silk, and in a tarot bag or a box.

CREATING A SPACE FOR YOUR READINGS

First, find a peaceful space you feel relaxed and comfortable in. Make sure your space has a flat, clean surface you can lay your cards on. Most readers put down a reading cloth first to protect the cards both physically, as well as energetically, from direct contact with the surface you're working on. The reading cloth is usually the silk cloth you wrap your cards in when they're not in use, but any piece of fabric you like will do.

SHUFFLING THE DECK

After you've cleansed the deck, shuffle the cards for a few moments. Relax and allow your feelings and questions to surface. To choose the cards for a reading, you can either use the fan method or cut the deck. The fan method is best when you want just a few cards for a reading, while cutting the deck suits more elaborate layouts that need lots of cards, such as the Celtic Cross.

FAN METHOD

WHEN READING FOR YOURSELF: Spread all the cards facedown in a fan shape. Choose the cards one by one with just your left hand (known as the hand of fate), from anywhere in the fan, and place them in front of you, still facedown, following the spread layout you have chosen.

WHEN READING FOR ANOTHER PERSON: Have the person shuffle the deck. Take the deck from the recipient and fan out the cards for him or her. Ask the recipient to choose the cards from the fan with his or her left hand and pass them to you so you can lay them out, keeping the cards facedown.

CUTTING THE DECK

WHEN READING FOR YOURSELF: Cut the deck twice with your left hand so you have three piles facedown on the table. Choose one pile to become the top of the deck and gather up the other two piles underneath it. Lay out the cards according to the spread you have chosen by dealing the cards from the top of the deck and placing them facedown in front of you.

WHEN READING FOR ANOTHER PERSON: Ask the recipient to shuffle the cards. Have the recipient split the deck into three piles using his or her left hand and then choose one pile. Gather up the remaining two piles for the person and place their chosen pile on top. Then you lay out the cards.

TURNING OVER THE CARDS

When turning over the cards, always flip them sideways—from left to right—not from top to bottom or vice versa, or you may be turning the card upside down. Doing so can give it a different meaning.

USING THE CARD INTERPRETATIONS

Consider the cards before you look up their meaning; think about what aspect of a card you are drawn to first. This is your internal guidance directing you to the most relevant meaning of the card for your reading. This also means that the cards can offer a varying significance each time you look at them. Similarly, when you read for other people, you will find that you don't give a card the same interpretation for every person who gets that card in a reading—you are personalizing the reading according to your intuition.

SOMETIMES YOU'LL BEGIN A READING AND CAN'T MAKE SENSE OF WHAT THE CARDS ARE TELLING YOU. IF THIS HAPPENS, HERE'S WHAT TO DO:

SHUFFLE AND LAY OUT THE CARDS AGAIN. If the same or similar cards come up this time, go with the reading. Relax and tune in to the card images; don't worry about reading the traditional interpretations. Say what comes into your head straight away, and the words will flow.

DID THE TEN OF WANDS COME UP? If so, this often means there's too much going on just now and it's not the right time to read your cards. Wait a day or two and try again.

IF YOU'RE READING FOR SOMEONE ELSE, feeling blocked can indicate the recipient's state of mind. If this happens, acknowledge the recipient's feelings and begin the reading again, asking him or her to let go of expectations.

WHAT ABOUT REVERSALS?

You will see that all the card interpretations in this book contain both upright and reversed card meanings. With a few exceptions, a reversed card's meaning is generally more negative than the positive, or upright, meaning. However, many tarot professionals ignore reversals in a reading and just turn the cards the right way up if they come out reversed; they use their intuition to interpret the card in a positive or negative light. Do whatever feels right for you.

GETTING INTUITIVE

Each card is full of symbols—but you will find that you notice one or two features that really stand out in each picture. These are what I call your intuition hooks. Once you hone in on these, go deeper and connect with how they make you feel. Don't worry about the written card meanings in this book just yet. Say whatever comes to your mind straight away—before you begin to think about what the symbols mean—and imagine yourself telling a story.

To develop the reading, try looking at the quick-reference meanings only (see pages 15 and 61) and then go back to the card images. Staying with the image as long as you can stimulates your intuition, which is essential to a reading, whereas reading the words engages your logical left brain, which often becomes the judge, questioning if you've got it "right."

There's no right or wrong—just your interpretation. You can read the detailed card meanings when you're not giving a reading to develop knowledge. But to begin with, look at the pictures first; this technique can help you read any deck of cards, not just Rider-Waite tarot.

CARD LAYOUTS

Readers often learn the Past, Present, Future; the Celtic Cross; and the Week Ahead card layouts as their foundation. Try them all and see which you prefer.

PAST, PRESENT, FUTURE

This easy spread is perfect for mini-readings. Shuffle the deck, fan the cards or cut the deck, and then lay three cards as shown:

1. Past Influences **2.** Present Situation **3.** Outcome

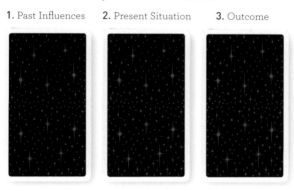

For more insight, you can lay an extra card for each position.

You can also create your own three-card reading to look at different life aspects—for example, Mind, Body, Spirit; or Love, Money, Home. You can also lay a card known as a Significator. A Significator is a card that first sums up the theme of a reading that you then lay down. For example: If you'd like to lay cards on one theme, such as love, you can choose an appropriate Significator from the deck, rather than laying it out randomly as the first card that comes up after shuffling. **FOR A LOVE READING, YOU MIGHT TAKE OUT THE LOVERS CARD AND THEN SHUFFLE THE DECK AND LAY DOWN THREE CARDS AROUND IT AS FOLLOWS:**

THE LOVERS **1.** Past Influences **2.** Present Situation **3.** Outcome

THE WEEK AHEAD

For a look at the Week Ahead, lay down one card for each day—though not in the regular, chronological sequence.

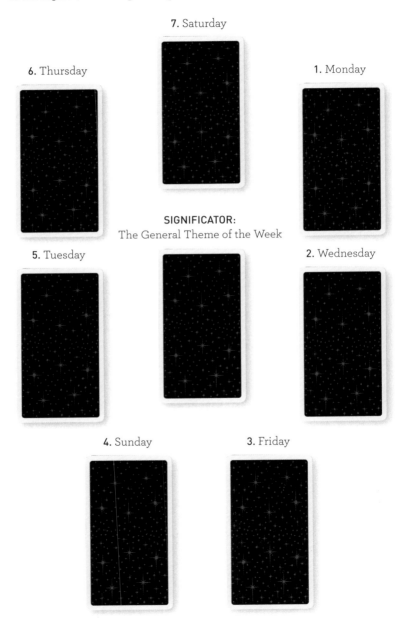

7. Saturday

6. Thursday

1. Monday

SIGNIFICATOR:
The General Theme of the Week

5. Tuesday

2. Wednesday

4. Sunday

3. Friday

THE CELTIC CROSS

The Celtic Cross is one of most popular tarot spreads in use today because it answers a question or, if you don't have an immediate question, gives an overview of your life just now. Set your intention before you begin, asking your question or for an overview as your shuffle.

SHUFFLE AND CHOOSE THE CARDS AND THEN LAY THEM OUT AS SHOWN BELOW.

TIP: If the tenth card is a court card—a Page, Knight, Queen, or King—then the outcome of the question is up to you or the person you are reading for.

1. You/The Situation in Question
2. What Crosses or Complements You
3. The Best That Can Be Achieved in the Circumstances
4. The Foundation: The Reason for the Reading
5. The Past
6. The Near Future
7. You
8. Your Environment—External Influences Affecting You
9. Hopes or Fears
10. The Outcome

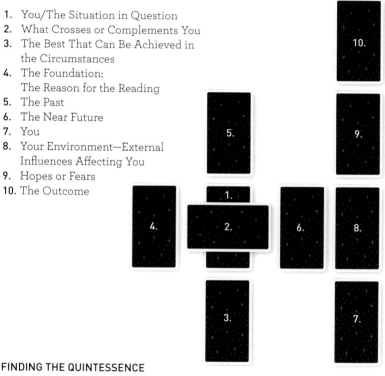

FINDING THE QUINTESSENCE

When you've finished a reading using any layout, here's a way to glean further insight: Add up the major arcana cards by number and then reduce it to a single digit. For example, if you had three cards—II, The High Priestess; XXI, The World; and XIV, Temperance—this gives 2 + 21 + 14 = 37. Reduce this number further by adding its two digits together: 3 + 7 = 10, or X, The Wheel of Fortune. The meaning of this card—a change for the better—offers an additional dimension.

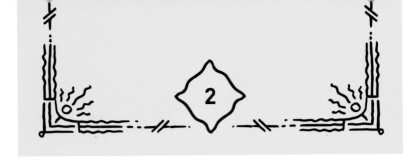

CARD INTERPRETATIONS: THE MAJOR ARCANA

A standard tarot deck has seventy-eight cards, divided into two groups: twenty-two major arcana cards and fifty-six minor arcana cards. The word arcana means secret. The major arcana denote important life events or shifts, while the minor arcana cards reflect day-to-day events. The minor arcana cards can be seen as being more detailed aspects of the major arcana cards.

Numbered from 0 (The Fool) to XXI (The World), the twenty-two major arcana cards can be referred to singularly as arcanum and collectively as keys or trumps.

If you're a beginner, you may want to start by using just the major arcana cards and progress to the full seventy-eight-card deck when you're more confident. The major arcana are the prime energies, whereas the minors are more incidental influences. As many minor cards are dilutions of the majors, you won't be missing out on any vital information by beginning with majors-only readings. The majors will give you or the person you are reading for the essential messages.

0 THE FOOL

KEY MEANINGS: Innocence, risk, and beginnings

UPRIGHT MEANING

The upright Fool signifies calculated risk. It's never too late to begin anew and follow your heart's desire. The journey ahead is not without danger, but it is time to take a leap of faith. This card augers well for those embarking on new enterprises and educational courses, provided sensible planning is in place; this is a time for optimism and a fresh perspective.

The Fool brings an opportunity to start over and feel young again or excited at the prospect of a new way of living; the Fool is an embodiment of your spirit, whether male or female, ready to explore and discover. Whatever you start now will go well, provided you do look before you leap—but once the decision is made, it's time to push forward and not look back; have courage, commit to your path, and be fully in the moment. The Fool's appearance in a reading can bring a sigh of relief, in that there is now a way ahead. Welcome in the new and travel lightly.

HERE ARE SOME INSIGHTS THE FOOL CAN OFFER IN PARTICULAR AREAS OF LIFE:

HOME: The Fool can show a young person leaving home for the first time. Also, surprise visitors could call. You may also have younger guests in your home.

RELATIONSHIPS: A new relationship—go with the flow at this point.

CAREER AND MONEY: You may have sabbatical or a new opportunity in your current job or a new career or enterprise. Prioritizing your workload is also the key to moving ahead swiftly.

REVERSED MEANING

Is what you're proposing—or a situation offered to you—a leap too far? The Fool reversed brings out his irresponsible side, as his mouth works ahead of his brain. Without thinking through the downsides, the Fool makes decisions that are not wise. The reversed Fool leaps without awareness and so becomes the literal idiot, sabotaging his chances due to desperation and irrationality. Think carefully before agreeing to a new approach to work and hold back from emotional commitments until you are sure of your ground.

HIS WISDOM MESSAGE

Leap, but look first.

I THE MAGICIAN

© 1990 U.S. Games Systems, Inc.

KEY MEANINGS: Action, creativity, and success

UPRIGHT MEANING

It's time for action—for communicating and expressing your ideas and desires. This is the card of the inventor, the traveler, the self-employed, and the entrepreneur, as it beckons you to broaden your horizons. You will have the drive to spur your plans forward, and, perhaps, to take new, creative approaches: to think laterally, ask questions, trust your internal guidance, and let go of procrastination.

Blessed with a magic wand, you have the ability to transform whatever you choose, and in this way, the Magician is a very positive card in a reading. He directs you to make the most of your skills and talents and step into your power; focus on your projects and capitalize on your personal strengths. Spiritually, the Magician shows you connecting with your higher, or true, self and acting with pure intention.

This card can also show a significant journey.

HERE ARE SOME OTHER POSSIBILITIES:

HOME: A house sale is completed, or you decide it is time to move forward with remodeling plans. This is a sociable time, with lots of visitors and entertaining.

RELATIONSHIPS: If you are single and want love, it is coming. If you are in a relationship, the Magician shows love in action, so you will begin to see commitment. Communication between you is excellent and you reach an even deeper understanding of each other's needs. The card can also show you acting as one, so a joint project may be on the horizon, too.

CAREER AND MONEY: There will be a new beginning, either finding new employment or a new direction in your existing work. This card can also show inspired leadership from a grounded and enthusiastic individual.

REVERSED MEANING

When the good Magician is reversed, he turns trickster, so this card can show you being misled by a charming manipulator. What you see is not what you get, and it's all show, not truth. In your projects, the Magician reversed can show a creative block as you feel torn between two paths or choices that get in the way of progress. It's time to choose one option and commit to it fully. The reversed card can also reveal delays to travel plans and miscommunication in general.

HIS WISDOM MESSAGE

Manifest your desires.

II THE HIGH PRIESTESS

KEY MEANINGS: Secrets, wisdom, and the spiritual world

UPRIGHT MEANING

Hidden knowledge, intuition, psychic experience, and significant dreams are the gifts of the High Priestess. This is a time for incubation and privacy, to go inward, deepening your relationship with your higher self and trusting your internal knowing. In your everyday life, confidentiality is key. If you have a secret, or a project you are nurturing, it is better to keep your own counsel.

On your spiritual path, the High Priestess predicts learning and a mentor. As the card of psychic gifts (along with card X, The Wheel of Fortune), her arrival in your reading can be a sign to follow your intuition and connect with your guides. If the High Priestess shows up in one of your first tarot readings, this is often a sign that tarot is part of your spiritual journey.

HERE ARE SOME OTHER SIGNS SHE CAN REVEAL:

HOME: It's a quiet time. Relations between family members may be calm but a little distant; you may be buried in your separate lives just now.

RELATIONSHIPS: This can mean being single for a time or, if you are in a relationship, you or your partner choosing to keep a part of your life separate, or secret.

CAREER AND MONEY: Success is coming, but contracts and new work are taking time to nurture. You can only be patient.

REVERSED MEANING

When reversed, the High Priestess can show an inappropriate mentor or choosing a temporarily wrong path. You might be listening to bad advice or someone might try to persuade you to go against your intuition. It can also indicate secrets that need to be out in the open; knowledge locked up too long may be potentially harmful.

HER WISDOM MESSAGE

Explore your spiritual side.

III THE EMPRESS

KEY MEANINGS: Abundance, generosity, and creativity

UPRIGHT MEANING

The gifts of the Empress are abundance and material comfort, sensuality and security, and emotional support. This is an auspicious card for children and families, showing harmony at home; if you are hoping to begin a family, the Empress symbolizes fertility and femininity. Your creative projects thrive and you prosper financially now, too. The Empress is resourceful, so when she appears in your reading, you can feel assured that your needs will be met. This card, therefore, shows the influence of a nurturing mother figure who supports you. As the you/your situation card in a reading, it reveals you are a good mother to others—and to yourself.

HERE ARE SOME ADDITIONAL POSSIBILITIES:

HOME: Renovation and extensions, home improvements; considering a move to a larger home; tending a garden.

RELATIONSHIPS: Happiness—If single, this indicates a good time to begin a relationship. Harmonious relationships exist within the family.

CAREER AND MONEY: Security; money flows—In work, you are resourceful, able to support others, and come up with inventive ways to manage your projects.

REVERSED MEANING

When reversed, the Empress shows financial issues and domestic strife. This may take the form of a controlling and disruptive influence at home. She can also show a creative block in your projects and someone who is needy and takes too much from you. The result of these challenges and demands is stressful, and there may be an impact on fertility if this is an issue for you now—literally in terms of conceiving a child or figuratively in terms of finding the time and peace of mind to grow an idea.

HER WISDOM MESSAGE

Life is abundant.

IV THE EMPEROR

KEY MEANINGS: Control, security, order, and ambition

UPRIGHT MEANING

In a reading, the Emperor can denote a powerful man, and the traditional male aspects of rulership and ambition. As the consort of card III, The Empress, he signifies the husband or other intimate partner who is constant and trustworthy. He is in control of his emotions, and comfortable with who he is. Less appealing, perhaps, is his need for conformity. Although he may have ambition, tradition is essential to his happiness.

As a general influence or symbol of the self, he brings balance, security, and conventional values. He reveals mastery of life and control over territory, and predicts that problems can be overcome with careful planning and single-mindedness. He shows a return to order, so his arrival in your reading is a welcome sign of improvement in your circumstances. You may also be offered protection from someone you trust; you can also trust yourself to make the right decisions.

It's time to live in the here and now, and use what practical resources you possess—wisdom, determination, and the skills of others—to realize your next steps. Be the leader.

HERE'S WHAT HE REPRESENTS IN SPECIFIC AREAS OF YOUR LIFE:

HOME: Order and smooth running. However, it is also important to set boundaries and protect what is yours.

RELATIONSHIPS: A new partner, or focusing on practical matters and future planning in established partnerships. Loyalty in love.

CAREER AND MONEY: Finances get organized and you plan how to balance expenditures. You can expect to have fairness at work and to be sure of your goals; you will either enjoy this new structure or feel it stifles your creativity.

REVERSED MEANING

When reversed, the Emperor is power-hungry and excessive in his demands, and represents the negative traits associated with traditional masculinity, such as being domineering, controlling, and even cruel. Greed is another aspect of the Emperor reversed. Whereas the upright Emperor knows his boundaries, the reversed Emperor does not know where to draw the line and may use excessive force or persuasion to get what he wants. This card therefore shows issues with authority figures and other potentially domineering individuals who are run by their egos.

HIS WISDOM MESSAGE

Take control; you are protected.

V THE HIEROPHANT

KEY MEANINGS: Education, unity, spiritual direction

UPRIGHT MEANING

In the upright position, the Hierophant shows support, self-realization, and expansion. This is a time to develop emotionally and spiritually—to commit to relationships; to think and philosophize; and to become more spiritually aware. In this way, the Hierophant offers an opportunity to integrate mind and spirit and ascend to a higher plane of awareness. Day to day, this means nurturing your talents through learning and heeding good advice.

While the Hierophant offers wise counsel, he does represent institutions and traditional values—which may be a comfort to you or a test of how much you are willing to conform. Even if his conventions are not for you, the Hierophant offers an opportunity to question and define your values.

As a spiritual leader, the Hierophant shows you the path to follow in a community, such as joining a study group or class through which you may learn a new skill. He also represents good judgment and fairness: The Hierophant asks you to tune your moral compass, so if you have been questioning a decision, it is time to do what is right.

HERE'S WHAT ELSE THE HIEROPHANT CAN SYMBOLIZE:

HOME: Expanding your current property; inviting people into your home to share your interests.

RELATIONSHIPS: Committed partnerships; marriage; celebrating the sacred in your relationship.

CAREER AND MONEY: Progress in your organization; direction and decisions; inspired leadership and growth.

REVERSED MEANING

When reversed, the Hierophant shows poor leadership. You may be misled by an incompetent or egotistic individual at work or on your spiritual path. This is the card of the bad guru—the judgmental teacher who is more interested in furthering his ambitions than supporting you in yours. In work, the Hierophant reversed can also show institutions that need restructuring: poor advice, mistrust, and wrong decisions with moral repercussions. It is better to seek your own path than to stay with a mentor or plan that doesn't suit your needs. Be a free spirit.

HIS WISDOM MESSAGE

Make the most of your gifts.

VI THE LOVERS

KEY MEANINGS: Love and relationships, maturity, and decisions

UPRIGHT MEANING

The Lovers show relationships and a decision. The card can predict meeting a new partner or a career opportunity, and your choice now will have a significant effect on your future. In the upright position, the person coming into your orbit now has a positive influence and offers true love—provided you follow the guidance of your heart rather than your head. If you are willing to take a risk rather than stay with a safe choice, you may soon discover your own Garden of Eden, which is fertile and rich with possibility.

If you are already in a relationship, a decision whether to take your partnership to a deeper level will be made. The issue that the Lovers card raises is your ability to make a decision based on your long-term future rather than short-term gains. In this way, you are being asked to make a mature decision that supports your true needs—respect, intimacy, love, and trust—and to connect with a partner who is emotionally available to you. Whatever your situation, the message is to follow your heart's desire.

AN ADDITIONAL MEANING OF THE LOVERS CARD IS A YOUNG PERSON LEAVING HOME AND MAKING INDEPENDENT DECISIONS.

HOME: If you're not living in your dream home, now is the time to work toward a property and location that will support your dreams and desires.

RELATIONSHIPS: A love decision—Look at your patterns in previous relationships and see what your current love, or prospective new partner, can offer you that is different and ultimately more fulfilling. If you are single, love yourself first to manifest the right relationship when the time comes.

CAREER AND MONEY: Career choices—One option may seem easier, but look carefully to ensure you are making the best decision in the long term. Look beyond money to your future development and ambitions.

REVERSED MEANING

When the Lovers card reverses, relationships go out of balance and the shadow side of your personalities enters the equation. A relationship is in crisis, and you may question your initial attraction as the values you once held as a couple feel corrupted. There may be inequality, betrayal, and dishonesty. The Lovers reversed is also an aspect of card XV, The Devil, which reveals lust, materialism, and addiction to negative patterns.

THEIR WISDOM MESSAGE

Follow the wisdom of your heart.

VII THE CHARIOT

KEY MEANINGS: Determination, victory, and a journey

UPRIGHT MEANING

The upright Chariot signifies success and a major departure. This is a time for determination and focus as you travel in a new direction. A decision is made, and now you can begin to experience real progress in your affairs. Ready to take control and navigate your path, you are poised to learn as your horizons rapidly expand. Just as the charioteer has his wand to drive him onward, you will need willpower to fuel your desires.

The Chariot can indicate a move or an important journey, and, on a mundane level, it shows you driving a car on your travels or getting a new vehicle.

FOLLOWING ARE SOME OTHER POSSIBILITIES:

HOME: Travel away from home is the focus now, rather than on extending or improving your home. You may also welcome travelers from other states or countries. Any disagreements with those you live with will be quickly overcome.

RELATIONSHIPS: A relationship progresses at a pace; if the cards around the Chariot show endings, you may be moving on alone—but this is your rightful path.

CAREER AND MONEY: Swift progress in business affairs—the opportunity coming your way will be challenging and exciting. Financially, you are on the road to success.

REVERSED MEANING

When reversed, there is arrogance and self-indulgence. This can show a person or event spiraling out of control. Ego is at work, and selfish needs come before the greater good, so the Chariot reversed can indicate recklessness and poor leadership. When the Chariot reverses and is tipped off the road, travel plans and house moves are disrupted or delayed.

HIS WISDOM MESSAGE

Take charge and reach for the stars.

VIII STRENGTH

KEY MEANINGS: Patience, tension, and strength

UPRIGHT MEANING

Strength shows that you turn to your higher self for self-guidance; she also demonstrates strength of character when dealing with pressure. Courage, determination, and patience are needed now, as it is time to get a situation—or individual—under control. You will need to act with grace and sensitivity, however, rather than using brute force. This is a good card for leadership, as it signifies you are ready to take on a challenge and stand firm; others may resist, but be consistent in your actions and results will come. In creative projects, Strength shows you taking a raw idea and developing it. You refine it without sacrificing its spirit or depleting your energy. This concept may take physical form as a document, piece of artwork, or prototype.

On a psychological level, Strength shows the integration of masculine and feminine traits and finding balance between the two. In terms of health, Strength shows resilience and vitality, recovery from illness, and the willpower to break bad habits.

HERE ARE SOME SPECIFICS:

HOME: There's a need to support and direct those with strong opinions. You may need to take the role of mediator.

RELATIONSHIPS: The need for balance—there is a danger that physical attraction masks emotional or other commitment issues that need to be addressed. This card is also a message of hope if your relationship has been tested, as the situation will soon improve.

CAREER AND MONEY: Tension at work—resolution comes gently and without force.

REVERSED MEANING

When reversed, Strength turns to weakness of will and avoidance of risk, conflicts, and decision-making. This can refer to you ignoring your instincts altogether or allowing fear of conflict to stop you from taking action. This avoidance is holding back your personal growth; in this situation, you can only learn through experience. Whatever you resist persists, so take charge and take on the challenge.

Strength reversed is an obvious message about weakness, so be aware that indolence and overthinking can be more exhausting than confrontation.

HER WISDOM MESSAGE

With strength, you can discover your higher purpose.

IX THE HERMIT

KEY MEANINGS: Healing and self-exploration

UPRIGHT MEANING

There's an opportunity to take time away from routine to consider your options or advance a personal project. This card can show you enjoying solitude, as you need space to process your thoughts and feelings. The Hermit can show a physical journey, but more commonly he represents a state of mind in which you wisely withdraw and keep your own counsel. It can show breaking with tradition and finding a unique approach to a challenge. You may appreciate a mentor, and when you are ready, as the saying goes, the teacher will appear. Until that time, you have yourself to rely upon, and you do have the answers; all you need is the mental space to connect with your inner wisdom. If you are under pressure to make a decision, the Hermit shows you need more time.

There is also a healing aspect to the Hermit, and the card can appear in a reading to show self-healing and healing others. You may need to guide others and show them the way forward. Even if you are not entirely sure you can help, you are equipped to do so.

THE HERMIT CAN ALSO INDICATE THE FOLLOWING:

HOME: Consider all your options carefully and avoid making big decisions at present. Prioritize your tasks and focus on planning rather than immediate action.

RELATIONSHIPS: Take time to invest in your current relationship or to work on your relationship with yourself. The card can also show a period of being single.

CAREER AND MONEY: Take a different approach and stand back. You may be drawn to research and professional development courses now. A mentor may guide you.

REVERSED MEANING

When reversed, you may be feeling alone and unsupported. However, this is more an attitude than reality, so it's worth asking yourself if you are avoiding help. The card can also show accepting a role—perhaps victim or martyr—that you find hard to let go of due to habit or stubbornness. Alternatively, the card can show a time when you are cut off from your usual support systems or have been unfriended by those you trusted. If this chimes for you, go with the upright card meaning and withdraw for a while, relying on your own guidance.

HIS WISDOM MESSAGE

Live quietly for a time.

X THE WHEEL OF FORTUNE

KEY MEANINGS: Fate, change, intuition

UPRIGHT MEANING

When the Wheel is upright, anything is possible—and usually positive. Chance meetings, unexpected offers, and news arrive in force. If life has been difficult recently, the Wheel shows a turn for the better.

Under this influence, your intuitive powers heighten, and you may find yourself tuning in to people from the past—who magically reappear. This is also an auspicious card for communication with family and friends who live some distance away. Additionally, the Wheel reveals psychic ability, either within you or someone close, and a chance to discover all your hidden aspects—both light and dark. You can use the Wheel's positive message wisely now to listen to your intuition and also to manifest your wishes, as your energy aligns with your guides, angels, and other spirit helpers who help you on your path. Your quest for knowledge is heightened now and, while you cannot control the forces of the universe, you can certainly come to a better understanding of your role within the universe.

THE WHEEL ALSO SUGGESTS THE FOLLOWING:

HOME: An unexpected change in your living arrangements will happen; it will be surprising but beneficial in the long term.

RELATIONSHIPS: An ex-partner or love interest comes back, but you will need to decide if this time your relationship will succeed. Don't try to make it work; if it is right, love will go smoothly.

CAREER AND MONEY: News is coming that will improve your situation. However, you will need to prioritize the demands upon youself and quickly adapt to new challenges.

REVERSED MEANING

When the Wheel is reversed, you may suffer some bad luck, but thankfully this marks the end of a run of challenges. In this way, the simple interpretation of the reversed Wheel is closure. The benefits of the upright Wheel will come—it will just take a little longer to gather momentum and move you forward. On a spiritual level, this card can also show a lack of confidence in your intuitive messages or a false start when choosing a way to spiritually develop. Vow to adapt, begin again, and keep on working toward your goal.

ITS WISDOM MESSAGE

Surrender to fate.

XI JUSTICE

KEY MEANINGS: Balance, perception, and objectivity

UPRIGHT MEANING

There will be a positive outcome. This is a time when past errors or imbalances can be redressed. You benefit from a fair system, provided you are accountable, honest, and deserving. Equally, you may be the judge in your own life, using your perspective and integrity to make good decisions that will safeguard your future. You may take a moral stand on an issue that affects you and those around you. In legal matters, a decision is made or a ruling given, which goes in your favor; justice will be done and order restored. On a spiritual level, Justice shows the working out of karma, or actions and consequences.

Justice shows a logical, considered influence. It is a welcome arrival in your reading if life has felt chaotic. It is a card of empowerment, advising you to take a left-brain approach to take control. Influential people favor you now, and your projects get support. Listen to advice from people around you whom you respect.

JUSTICE CAN ALSO INDICATE THE FOLLOWING:

HOME: Legal issues concerning property are resolved. Contracts are signed and you can make progress.

RELATIONSHIPS: While balance and practical issues are important now, take care that your emotional needs are met. Find the right balance between work and relationships.

CAREER AND MONEY: At work you may be tested, but the outcome is positive; job interviews and negotiations are successful. Financially, you are coming to the end of a frugal period—money matters are set to improve.

REVERSED MEANING

Life goes out of balance as work, relationships, and money issues spiral out of control. A decision may go against you, so there may be dishonesty or a miscarriage of justice. You are treated unfairly, which is compounded by bad advice from a trusted individual. You are not able to speak your truth and feel overruled by those who don't understand your predicament. It is important to find your voice and stay strong to your values—if you are in the right.

HER WISDOM MESSAGE

With the right values, reward comes.

XII THE HANGED MAN

KEY MEANINGS: Waiting, sacrifice, and enlightenment

UPRIGHT MEANING

The obvious meaning of the card at first glance is hanging around: Events are not moving with speed, but all you can do is wait patiently in the knowledge that the universe has its own plan. The card can also indicate that you may have made sacrifices just now and are eager to see rewards. Unfortunately, you cannot force an outcome that fits with your timetable. There are many other factors about which you can have no knowledge or influence. Therefore, you may also expect delays to travel plans and projects. On a creative level, this card can appear frequently when a person is feeling frustrated with their progress. However, the message of the Hanged Man is incubation—your project needs time to evolve. Use this time to develop perspective on your work and your ambitions.

Another message from the Hanged Man is to try to see things from a new angle. If your approach isn't working, ask yourself if you can think laterally or find a way to turn a situation around.

THE HANGED MAN CAN ALSO SUGGEST THE FOLLOWING:

HOME: Waiting and delays may affect remodeling or house moves. Try to invest your time wisely while you wait—there may be a creative solution.

RELATIONSHIPS: You are unable to get the commitment you need from a partner, or you may be the one unwilling to commit. Traditionally, it can also show hanging around for a lover to acknowledge you as a partner rather than friend. If you're waiting too long, you may decide it's not worth the emotional investment.

CAREER AND MONEY: Hold back on signing contracts or dealing with legal matters just now. With work, decisions may be going on that will affect your position, but you are protected. If you are looking for work, there may be delays and frustration.

REVERSED MEANING

The Hanged Man reversed can be a sign of rigid thinking and martyrdom. You may need to revise your expectations; what you think you want may not be possible. In the position, the card asks you if you are hanging on to a fantasy that may make you a victim rather than a victor. Take another view and liberate yourself from a contract or other obligation that cannot offer you what you want.

HIS WISDOM MESSAGE

Use your time wisely.

XIII DEATH

KEY MEANINGS: Transformation and change

UPRIGHT MEANING

Death brings endings and beginnings—sometimes all at once. This a time of fast and deep transformation and an opportunity to let go of whatever you no longer need. Unlike card XX, Judgment, which signals a process of self-examination, Death's impact is sudden and may be shocking. You have little control over external events when Death looms, but in time you will be able to see this sharp change in circumstances as a blessing. A break with the past—from relationships and friendships to work that is no longer satisfying—is the only way forward. In this sense, Death can be a release and a relief. Death, after all, is the ultimate reality check, and he leaves you with the bare bones, the truth.

IN CERTAIN AREAS OF LIFE, DEATH CAN SIGNIFY THE FOLLOWING:

HOME: You need to find a new home; the place you are living no longer meets your needs. New circumstances may offer an opportunity to relocate.

RELATIONSHIPS: A relationship ends or there is a period of necessary separation. In friendships, there will be an opportunity to reconnect when the time is right.

CAREER AND MONEY: Signifying a career change or the ending of business partnerships or ways of bringing in an income, Death also suggests new opportunities are on the horizon. Financially, this is a tough time, but money matters will improve, so hold tight.

REVERSED MEANING

Death reversed has virtually the same meaning as the card in the upright position, but the difference is in your reaction. You may feel anxious and stressed, unable to comprehend what is happening, rather than being accepting. When Death is reversed, the universe is telling you that there is no way back—a relationship cannot be mended, or an employer won't change their mind. If you do a second reading and ask the question again, this card can appear after you have already had Death upright, as a final confirmation of your question.

ITS WISDOM MESSAGE

Swift change brings new beginnings.

XIV TEMPERANCE

KEY MEANINGS: Moderation, reconciliation, healing, and angelic guidance

UPRIGHT MEANING

Temperance shows you dealing with a potentially volatile situation, and you need to temper your thoughts and actions to find balance and harmony. This means choosing neither one nor the other, but blending two opposing forces to create an inspired solution. The card also asks you not to resist, but to accept both sides of a situation and be guided by what feels most natural to you. It is time to reconcile any area of your life that is out of kilter. Be hands-on; you can analyze what you might do for eons, but what matters now is action.

Temperance also shows you are connecting with your guides and angels. You may be given a sign, such as advice from a friend or even a stranger whom the angels have sent to help you. This may also be the beginning of a spiritual journey for you. In your projects, what you imagine you can create. You may also be inspired by an invention or work of art from the past.

HERE ARE SOME OTHER INTERPRETATIONS:

HOME: Running a household and dealing with demanding children or partners is a fine balancing act, but you have the financial and emotional resources to succeed.

RELATIONSHIPS: This is a stage in a relationship when you can reach a new level of trust. If you are single, you may be guided toward a new partner; it's an emotionally intense time.

CAREER AND MONEY: You may be dealing with difficult or highly sensitive individuals. Be the diplomat, and you can work a miracle. In money terms, pay extra attention to your income and outgoings.

REVERSED MEANING

Temperance reversed shows imbalance and unfairness in relationships and problems with money; what you pour into your relationships and work isn't rewarded. This card can also show you struggling with change, and the past dominating your present and future. In this position, difficult old memories can resurface and you feel held back. Try to look at what you need now, in the present.

ITS WISDOM MESSAGE

You are guided to find peace.

XV THE DEVIL

KEY MEANINGS: Enslavement and temptation

UPRIGHT MEANING

You may be enslaved to an ideal or a relationship that demands too much. What started positively has reversed, and now you are seeing a situation for what it is. It is a destructive situation, and you may be feeling controlled and under a bad influence. This is a card of greed, temptation, and materialism. Yet to change the situation, you will need to think laterally and use a little cunning. It's never worth confronting the problem, as the negativity is endemic—hence the Devil card often appears to describe situations that are not worth trying to fix or heal. The message is to simply walk away, to escape in the best way you can, regardless of the temptation of staying.

The Devil often arrives in a relationship reading to show lust and negative ways of relating, in that one partner is gaining much more that the other. By extension of this, additional meanings of the Devil are addiction—issues with sex, food, substance abuse, and overall negative thinking patterns.

SOME OTHER SPECIFICS INCLUDE THE FOLLOWING:

HOME: Here, the Devil may indicate living with domineering people or dealing with a difficult landlord. Psychic vampires and generally negative people may drain your energy. You may feel controlled and invaded just now.

RELATIONSHIPS: Difficult relationships are indicated here, such as controlling partners, lust-over-love situations, affairs, and codependent patterns. For separated partners, the Devil may show financial dependency or other ongoing money or property issues that keep you tied to the past.

CAREER AND MONEY: You experience bad financial contracts, an unsatisfying career, domineering bosses, or a toxic work environment—but you stay because you are financially trapped.

REVERSED MEANING

When reversed, this is one of the few cards whose meaning becomes more hopeful. With the upright Devil, it's time to acknowledge how you may be trapped and to begin to search for the light. Reversed, the Devil suggests the decision will be easier than you think. When the card is upside down, the chains around the couple are more lax than they appear, so a situation is not quite as drastic as you first thought. Now is the time to make your move.

In terms of health, a difficult cycle is about to end. Addiction and bad habits become easier to manage and eventually banish, and you or those close to you can look forward to recovery.

HIS WISDOM MESSAGE

In one leap, you can be free.

XVI THE TOWER

KEY MEANINGS: Destruction and enlightenment

UPRIGHT MEANING

The Tower hits us with sudden change: the collapse of an ideal, a dream, an organization, or a relationship. This is inevitable and is due to forces beyond your control. The Tower can represent shattered ego, so you may feel vulnerable and confused. Yet you can only surrender to the power of the Tower and work on accepting the huge shift in awareness it offers—although the benefits may not be obvious just yet.

The upside of the Tower is its message of release. The walls come tumbling down, but in the moment of destruction, everything is illuminated. You can see inside the Tower and look at how you built it—how you lived in your psychological tower and what it protected you from. With the Tower gone, you can begin to sense how the future might evolve. What you build next can have more foundation.

Some readers find the Tower an apt descriptor of migraines, with the buildup of pressure and intense pain. The Tower's lightning bolt has also been likened to sexual tension and earth-shattering release.

HERE ARE SOME OTHER POSSIBILITIES THE TOWER MAY SIGNIFY:

HOME: The Tower can illustrate an abrupt change to your circumstances. A property you hoped to move into does not materialize, or you encounter delays to building projects, for example.

RELATIONSHIPS: A secret comes to light, which may be shocking. It is time to let go of past patterns. Equally, you may experience an intense physical or spiritual attraction, which has a profound impact on your orderly existence.

CAREER AND MONEY: Restructuring in businesses, possible redundancies that may mean a move—the Tower signifies change. A person in a position of power makes tough decisions, and a leader may be ousted from their post.

REVERSED MEANING

When the Tower is reversed, you may find yourself taking responsibility even when you are blameless. It can also show you have held on to a career, project, or relationship that is not strong enough to stand the test of time. If you have clung to the past to protect yourself from reality, your fears may materialize. The Tower's collapse is inevitable, so do not feel responsible. Its impact is sudden and dramatic, and soon you will know exactly where you stand.

ITS WISDOM MESSAGE

Surrender.

XVII THE STAR

KEY MEANINGS: Hope, guidance, inspiration, and creativity

UPRIGHT MEANING

The Star offers hope and guidance, so if things have felt difficult recently, have faith that your luck is about to change for the better. The Star is a powerful symbol of hope, and you can begin to appreciate everything life has to offer, including better physical and spiritual well-being. The Star supports beauty, and creativity flows like the star-maiden's water. In your projects and relationships, you can be fully expressed, sharing your love, gifts, and talents. The Star allows you to shine and show your Star quality, so your efforts are appreciated. You may also feel more intuitive and insightful under the Star's influence and have more trust in messages from your angels and guides.

The Star also shows good health. It is the card of the healer and is traditionally associated with astrology.

THE STAR CAN ALSO INDICATE THE FOLLOWING:

HOME: You feel inspired to create beauty and style in your home, so craft projects and design are especially favored now. If you have your eye on a dream home, it will come to you.

RELATIONSHIPS: The Star shows that you are destined to be with someone; it is time to find a soul mate. Other existing relationships are calm and harmonious.

CAREER AND MONEY: The Star brings money luck. Work you do begins to pay off, as you have considered your long-term goals and given attention to what matters most. Entrepreneurs may be guided to begin a new business, or you find you have a hidden talent you can put to good use. The Star can also show awards and fame.

REVERSED MEANING

In the reversed position, the Star can show giving up too easily in your projects and experiencing a creative block. You may be too attached to a fantasy scenario—after all, starlight is bewitching—while overlooking the details. Alternatively, you may feel lulled into a false sense of security in a venture that has no foundation and little chance of success. An additional meaning is feeling alone just now, without the support you need.

ITS WISDOM MESSAGE

Be inspired—dreams come true.

XVIII THE MOON

KEY MEANINGS: Illusion, dreams, and crisis

UPRIGHT MEANING

The Moon's traditional meaning is a crisis of faith and a period of emotional vulnerability. It reveals misgivings about a situation, as you cannot be sure if what you are seeing is the truth. Under the light of the Moon, is what you are seeing an illusion? Or does the Moon bring to light the essence of a problem that needs attention? This may be a time of deep emotional conflict, and the struggle is private rather than shared.

You have a decision to make, and to choose wisely, you need to rely on your senses rather than logic. Take note of your intuitive messages and dreams now and acknowledge them as valid sources of information that will lead you in the right direction. The Moon can show you being asked to take a risk, to broaden your life experience. The prospect may make you uncomfortable, but the Moon asks you to dive deep and examine the real cause of unrest.

THE MOON CAN ALSO SUGGEST THE FOLLOWING:

HOME: You could be feeling disillusioned about your current living situation or having second thoughts about a move or home improvement project that is proving costlier than anticipated. On a positive note, you may intuitively find an object you thought was lost.

RELATIONSHIPS: Confusion and disappointment reign as someone lets you down. A lack of trust that a relationship will work leads you to a love decision.

CAREER AND MONEY: You may achieve a goal but ultimately feel it was not worth the effort. With colleagues, emotions run high, and you may need to protect yourself from others' negativity. Money matters are stable, but you want more satisfaction from work than just the paycheck.

REVERSED MEANING

When the Moon is reversed, you may avoid difficult emotions and confrontations, so your needs are not expressed or recognized. A trauma is ignored again rather than explored, so the Moon reversed can show you going back to old ways of coping with the past. The card can also show you feeling stuck in an old emotional pattern that keeps arising—until you give it attention.

ITS WISDOM MESSAGE

Be guided by messages from your unconscious.

XIX THE SUN

KEY MEANINGS: Success, good health, and a holiday

UPRIGHT MEANING

The Sun brings success and achievement and is one of the most positive cards in the major arcana. If you have had a challenging time, the Sun shows that every aspect of your life will improve. You'll also enjoy more energy, and if you or someone close has suffered from health problems, the card predicts recovery and a return to good health. As a card of energy and growth, all your projects benefit now, so the Sun heralds a good time to nurture your creative endeavors, your business, and the relationships you value.

This card is also associated with children and family. It reveals good news about children in general and also about spending happy times with friends who make you smile. You may be reunited with an old friend, partner, or family member. In terms of a state of mind, the Sun shows you feeling carefree and creative, nurturing your inner child.

In a layout with "negative" cards, the Sun has the power to shed a positive light on the whole reading.

HERE'S SOME OTHER GOOD NEWS THE SUN CAN PREDICT:

HOME: You feel comfortable and secure in your home—you may also feel more like entertaining others. In particular, the Sun shows children coming into your home.

RELATIONSHIPS: Partnerships bloom under the sun as your relationship grows and you enjoy every minute together. You may also take a trip away to a sunny place to escape everyday pressures.

CAREER AND MONEY: The Sun does not specifically predict money but does show success and a position from which you can generate money. The Sun shines on your career, too, as you get the acknowledgment you deserve. Now is the time to bask in your success.

REVERSED MEANING

It's virtually impossible to see any negative side to the Sun, even when reversed. The only glitch could be a delay to travel plans, but you will enjoy a happy and content period regardless.

ITS WISDOM MESSAGE

Enjoy your success.

XX JUDGMENT

KEY MEANINGS: Assessment, and letting go of the past

UPRIGHT MEANING

It is time to come to a decision about the past. Great changes and opportunities are on the horizon, but before you can decide on your direction, certain past issues need to be addressed. This process is purely about how you judge yourself on your past actions and attitudes. In the upright position, Judgment shows you will feel you have acted with integrity and did the best you could. As you accept yourself fully, you can blow your own trumpet and praise yourself for your achievements. An additional meaning is being in the public eye, hence Fame, the card's alternative title.

Judgment also predicts a spiritual awakening, as you feel called to explore your potential. You have learned much about yourself in this most recent phase and are ready to go further, developing your spiritual connection with your guides and angels. As you receive guidance on your path, your confidence and wisdom will grow.

HERE'S MORE INSIGHT:

HOME: You may be drawn to an old property or consider returning to a place that holds happy memories. You will soon need to make a major property decision.

RELATIONSHIPS: Love is assessed and shifts into a new phase. There may be a need for reconciliation, if you deem the relationship worthwhile. If you are single, you may revisit an old relationship and decide if it is worth trying again. An old friend may reappear.

CAREER AND MONEY: Acknowledgment for your successes is coming; finances also improve.

REVERSED MEANING

When reversed, you may be stuck in the past or refuse to learn the lessons that are there for you. You may find yourself in old patterns and not yet able to break free. Delays are also indicated, in terms of future plans, and you may be feeling trapped and unable to progress, without really understanding why. You have the ability to judge your actions and attitudes and then move on; the past cannot be changed, only accepted. Have compassion for the person you were then and for the decisions you made. You don't have to live with the results of these choices in the future; you can decide to be free.

ITS WISDOM MESSAGE

Look back with pleasure.

XXI THE WORLD

KEY MEANINGS: Completion, success, reward, and joy

UPRIGHT MEANING

The upright card denotes triumph, completion, and reward for your efforts—and for this reason, the World is one of the most welcome cards in a reading. It denotes deep joy and happiness, and now you can really feel your deserved success. Cherished projects fly, as your commitment and dedication pays off. Life feels balanced, too, as work, relationships, finances, and domestic affairs run smoothly.

A phase is coming to an end in a positive way, and you will be acknowledged publicly for what you do. Now is the time to enjoy your fame, and you will have the confidence to take center stage. If you have been waiting for a decision or opportunity to manifest, the World will soon turn in your favor. You may also benefit spiritually just now, living more mindfully and from the heart.

This is also a time for celebration, and in a reading, the World often reveals anniversaries, birthdays, and parties, so it is a great card for groups and positive group consciousness. You may also decide to venture out into the world and travel far afield.

THE WORLD COULD ALSO MEAN THE FOLLOWING:

HOME: A dream-home come true—whatever you have worked toward can be yours now, whether it's successful building work or other remodeling.

RELATIONSHIPS: Happiness and joy; your relationship is fulfilling and loving.

CAREER AND MONEY: You're achieving your goals. An award at work, a new position and/or promotion—the World shows you rising in status and being given more authority. You may also receive gifts at this time.

REVERSED MEANING

When reversed, the World shows you are ready to move on but feel blocked or don't feel you are deserving of success. It can also show hanging on to one ambition that eludes you—and if so, it's time to redefine what you want and adjust your expectations, as you may be clinging on to a dream to the exclusion of all else. Alternatively, you may feel eclipsed by another's shining light. Overall, however, the negatives here are minor, and you will get what you deserve; it may just take a little longer to become obvious. In the meantime, keep the faith.

ITS WISDOM MESSAGE

Enjoy your success.

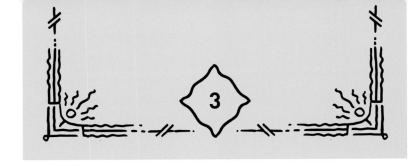

CARD INTERPRETATIONS: THE MINOR ARCANA

The remaining fifty-six cards are known collectively as the minor arcana, and they are arranged into four suits: Wands, Pentacles, Cups, and Swords. Each suit has fourteen cards, from Ace to Ten, plus four court cards: Page, Knight, Queen, and King.

THE FOUR SUITS CORRESPOND TO SPECIFIC AREAS OF LIFE:

CUPS: emotions and relationships

PENTACLES: property, money, and achievement

SWORDS: the intellect and decisions

WANDS: instinct, travel, and communication

ACE OF CUPS

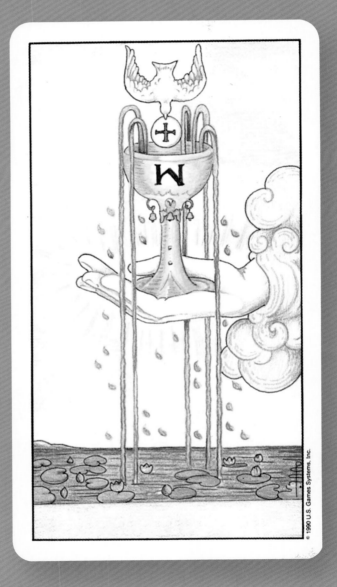

KEY MEANINGS: Love, relationships, and beginnings

UPRIGHT MEANING

The Ace of Cups brings the gift of love and key emotional events: fertility, pregnancy, birth, and motherhood; when not predicting a pregnancy, it can reveal that being a parent and/or partner takes priority over work, finances, and projects. In relationships, the card denotes falling in love, passion, and a significant new partnership. In existing relationships, it signifies love and support. Positive emotions flow.

If you are nurturing a new project, this Ace heralds creativity and growth, so make time for activities you enjoy, and you will see them flourish. An enterprise you hold dear will come to fruition, so it's time to turn to your novel, business concept, or travel plan and give it your full attention. This is also a great card for spiritual growth, so you may find yourself discovering a belief system or other important way to explore your spirituality.

Generally, this is a time for love, kindness, conviviality, and good friends, the simple joy in living each day and appreciating every moment.

In a reading, one Ace brings a focus on the life area according to the suit, which can set the theme of the reading. If two or more Aces appear near each other in a reading, it means the following:

> **TWO ACES:** An important partnership
>
> **THREE ACES:** Good news
>
> **FOUR ACES:** Excitement, beginnings, and potential

REVERSED MEANING

As you might expect from the meaning of the upright card, when reversed, the Ace suggests fertility issues and creative block. There may be lack of space and time to nurture your relationships and projects, or you may be the one feeling neglected; conversely, you may be feeling exhausted due to others' emotional demands. If you are asking about a new relationship, sadly, the reversed One can indicate disappointment and confusion—a potential new love does not develop into something more lasting.

In general, the reversed card reveals insecurity and doubt, and you may not feel you can believe in those people you'd like to trust. Follow your instincts and hold on to your self-belief; thankfully, this influence will not last.

TWO OF CUPS

KEY MEANINGS: Love and partnerships old and new

UPRIGHT MEANING

The Two of Cups represents harmony, peace, partnership, and love. In relationships, the card signifies a deeper commitment in an existing relationship, such as an engagement, moving in together, or getting married (particularly when it appears with the "marriage" cards, V, The Hierophant, and the Ten of Pentacles). There's a great connection between you two, so your emotions are freely expressed and reciprocated; you feel whole and content. The Two of Cups also predicts new romance and strong passions, which may be all-consuming just now. Inspiring partnerships are favored too, so this is an auspicious card for getting together with a study partner or anyone with whom you share similar creative interests, such as writing, crafting, and other hobbies, or psychic and healing work. Whomever you hook up with, the relationship will be mutually supportive and understanding.

If friendships have been difficult territory for you recently, the Two of Cups shows harmony will return, and in general, this Two shows reconciliation. Old arguments will be resolved as you put the past behind you. Any ongoing negotiations will go in your favor, too—contracts, financial settlements, custody issues, or rearranging your working hours or schedule, for example.

If the Two represents you in your reading, the focus is on feelings and your intuition. Nurture all your relationships and enjoy the love and pleasure they bring. As a prediction card, it shows love: Deeper love is coming—and you deserve all that is on offer.

REVERSED MEANING

When reversed, the Two reveals relationship stress. A new romance may turn sour as your hopes for love are disappointed. Also, the card asks you to rely on your intuition; there may be a secret you don't yet know, and traditionally, the reversed Two can show infidelity. Although on the surface everything may appear to be ticking along, pay attention to your instincts; there's a reason for doubt, and it's time to communicate openly about any fears rather than ignore them.

Generally, in established relationships, the Two can also indicate an unavoidable glitch simply due to the ongoing stresses and strains of leading too-busy lives. If it seems like this is the case, try to keep communicating— there may be a lack of understanding between you just now, but with work on both sides, you can rekindle your connection. Passion may be on hold just now, but it can return.

THREE OF CUPS

KEY MEANINGS: Celebration, abundance, family, and friendships

UPRIGHT MEANING

It's time to celebrate! The Three shows parties and reunions—from anniversaries, christenings, weddings, and birthdays to a great night out or weekend away with friends and family. This is a time for indulgence and reward, to enjoy other's company, be carefree, and have simple fun. There's also a flirtatious air about this Three, so if you're looking for a relationship, you'll soon be in the perfect situation and mood for lighthearted love.

The cups on the card are raised in a toast: There's a feeling of abundance, but if you're a wine- rather than water-drinker, or you've got a sweet tooth, you may be tempted to overindulge. However, whatever your pleasure, the Three ultimately reveals emotional and/or physical healing. Spending time with people who make you feel good raises your vibration and energy levels. This positive influence can also soothe physical ailments that are triggered or exacerbated by stress.

As three is the number of creation, this shows a creative time—literally, with a pregnancy or birth, or in your creative goals. Turn your focus to new ideas and share them, as whatever you do will be enjoyable and well received, and even rewarded, by others. It's time to let your talent shine.

REVERSED MEANING

When reversed, the Three of Cups can indicate a flirtation or indulgence gone too far, with affairs and heated emotions. In established relationships, there may be distance and a lack of cohesion and understanding. Someone close may be overly opinionated and egotistical, and the dynamics of a close relationship—romantic or friendship—become skewed. Emotional betrayal in friendships is also a common meaning of the Three of Cups.

Creativity takes a nosedive, too, as creative blocks abound; it may be hard to get started as you suffer a lack of motivation and support. If so, take a break and return to your projects when you feel more grounded and less affected by others' emotional demands.

This card can also show irritating or recurrent health problems that need your attention.

FOUR OF CUPS

KEY MEANINGS: Restlessnes and boredom

UPRIGHT MEANING

If you are looking for a relationship, the Four of Cups shows disillusion. This card often comes up if you have been hurt in the past and protect yourself with a checklist, instantly rejecting anyone who doesn't live up to your exacting standards—to the degree that even if your soul mate came along right now, you wouldn't recognize his or her potential. I call this the "Will I ever meet anyone I like?" card. The answer is: You can and will, but it's time to risk opening up emotionally again. You may think you're ready for love, but there may be some past issues still to heal. If you're in an established relationship, the Four of Cups shows a tinge of boredom. This may be a phase, and if so, it's time to inject some romance; otherwise, you may find yourself staying in a relationship out of habit.

In work and home life, the card shows a static situation—you may feel bored with your job or need to make a positive change to your environment. Even a small change will go a long way to making you feel you are going forward, so look around for some much-needed inspiration—it isn't far away.

REVERSED MEANING

The meaning of the reversed Four of Cups is generally the same as for the upright card, but with a higher degree of dissatisfaction—you may be yearning for change but don't yet know what you want. If so, it's important to try new tactics at work and address what needs to change in your relationship or environment. Try to express your needs now, rather than locking them up.

When the Four of Cups is reversed, the man's crossed legs echo the bent knee of card XII, The Hanged Man. One of this major arcana card's meanings is hanging around, feeling in limbo. Rather than wait for change, the message of the reversed Four of Cups is to take control and make life happen. Thankfully, this limbo is temporary—change is always possible.

FIVE OF CUPS

KEY MEANINGS: Loss, leaving, and sorrow

UPRIGHT MEANING

The Five of Cups is the card of upset and loss. It often shows sadness and confusion due to a breakup, disappointment or arguments in a close friendship, or the need to temporarily move away from a family member who has caused hurt. The card can also apply to leaving a job or home before you are ready to do so—you are forced to deal with whatever life throws your way, whether invited or not. This card can also refer to a loss of status or money. The gift of this Five is that there is no mistaking what has happened because you feel it in every bone of your body. At this point, there is no going back. But all is not lost: You will be able to move onward and upward regardless. The two remaining cups on the card can show the support of friends, family, and colleagues.

The Five of Cups can also come up in a reading for a bereavement and the natural sense of loss and grief this brings. It's also an indicator that you or the person you are reading for is revisiting the past, trying to assimilate old stress and sorrow in order to make a fresh start.

REVERSED MEANING

The Five of Cups along with major arcana card XV, The Devil, are the only two cards in the tarot deck whose reversed interpretations are more positive than their upright meanings. The Five reversed reveals you have already experienced the lowest point in a downward cycle and, as a result, are close to recovery, finally letting go of painful past memories. Ready to pick up the pieces, you will be stronger than you were before, able to face reality and move forward.

An additional meaning of the card is meeting up with old friends and, socially speaking, coming back to life.

SIX OF CUPS

KEY MEANINGS: Harmony, childhood,
reconciliation, and old friends

UPRIGHT MEANING

The Six of Cups reveals happy memories and a time to recall childhood with fondness. Your children, if you have them, may help you reconnect with your own childhood, or you are able to give your inner child free rein to play and have fun without the usual burden of worries. This is a time for good things coming from the past—reunion parties, reconnecting with old friends and more distant family members, or literally going back to your roots. This card may predict a trip home or to a place with fond memories. In some way, the past returns to help you in the present, too, as conversations and reminiscing with old friends or contacts seeds a new idea or approach.

Overall, you will find the right balance in relationships and enjoy a period of peace and harmony. This Six of Cups also shows compassion and kindness, so if you have suffered poor treatment, your situation is set to improve. Sweet, happy times are ahead, and any disruptions or upsets will be soothed and remedied.

In love, an old flame comes back, and you may need to weigh up if it is worth going back to the relationship.

REVERSED MEANING

When the Six of Cups is reversed, nostalgia rules, and you may recall past events with more positivity than they deserve. The card can also show you feeling locked in the past as a way to avoid moving on. A particular relationship needs to stay in the past rather than be revived. Unexpected visitors or communications may stir up old memories, and if so, let the memories rest—these people have no place in your future just now.

SEVEN OF CUPS

KEY MEANINGS: Opportunities and extremes

UPRIGHT MEANING

Choices and confusion—While the Seven brings the potential for amazing opportunities, these options and offers are insubstantial. At present, it's not clear what's feasible and what is fantasy, as everything feels up in the air, just like the floating cups on the card itself. Be discerning and find out what you can about each possible path, but ultimately you'll need to choose by paying attention to your instincts and emotions. This is not a test of logic: Go with the flow and trust your inner knowing. Don't rush. In relationships, the card can show new doorways opening again as joint finances improve.

The Seven is also the card of the visionary and shows the beginning stages of a new project, when anything is possible. Dreams and visions are additional interpretations.

REVERSED MEANING

The reversed Seven of Cups has much the same meaning as the upright card, but here, extreme emotions are in play. Be aware of the danger of idealizing a situation and avoiding a difficult truth; in relationships, the card can mean being deceived by appearances—a new lover may not be faithful. This is not the right time for commitment. Avoid becoming embroiled in drama; step back until your options are clear.

EIGHT OF CUPS

KEY MEANINGS: Departure, change, and emotional intelligence

UPRIGHT MEANING

The upright Eight of Cups reveals a time of restlessness when it feels as if something is missing. Work and relationships may appear harmonious from the outside, but your intuition is nagging you. The result may be a departure. Traditionally, the Eight of Cups predicts you leave a situation or break an agreement that no longer gives you fulfilment. This should not be a hasty decision; only move on when you are sure that there is no more you can gain or contribute. When the timing is right, there's also less drama than you would expect: Like the figure on the card slipping away in the night, you can take your leave quietly and swiftly. Naturally, you may feel sadness but little regret—provided the timing is right.

Like the figure in red following the path of the river, it's now time to go with the flow. You'll soon feel energized to move on to where your interests and curiosity call. You can also feel content with what you have achieved.

This card often turns up in a reading to show that you have already left a situation emotionally, and action will follow as you now take your actual leave. It can also predict a time to travel, to explore physically or through spiritual journeying.

REVERSED MEANING

What are you holding on to? Take stock: Are you clinging onto the past when you really do know that your current living situation has to change? When reversed, the Eight of Cups shows errors of judgment, so you jump too soon or stay too long, unable to see that there's an alternative way to do things. At this point, there's no logical solution; like the Eight of Cups' sphere of Hod, for the mind and its strategies, an intellectual approach might make you feel in control, but the way ahead is to follow your instincts. Timing is important now, so trust yourself that you will know the right time to move on, without self-pressure. An additional meaning of the card is being abandoned, leaving you confused as others move on from you—with undignified haste.

NINE OF CUPS

KEY MEANINGS: Happiness

UPRIGHT MEANING

The Nine of Cups is known as the wish card because it foretells a dream come true. Whatever you hope for can now come to fruition. Joy comes from prosperity, generosity, and optimism, alongside parties and entertainment.

In relationships, the Nine of Cups reveals new romance and rewarding friendships. Whatever feelings have been nurtured in the past can now be expressed as others show their hearts. The time for waiting for love is over; if love has grown, it will be declared fully. Friends will step closer to you as you feel more connected to your own heart. When fully living your truth, others respond. In the spirit of sharing, there is now an easy connection with others as projects begin and existing work becomes more rewarding. This is a time to communicate, laugh, and appreciate all you have.

If you are nurturing a new project or idea, the Nine of Cups heralds its growth, so listen to your intuition, make time for activities that make you happy, and see them flourish. Astrologically, this card is linked with Jupiter in Pisces, which promotes imagination, artistic flair, and generosity—so it is time to share and own your ideas. Independence is also important now.

The Nine also favors good health, as old tensions dissolve, flowing away in the waters of the past. Now is the time to appreciate the joy of the present.

REVERSED MEANING

When reversed, ego steps in—and with it self-centeredness and emotional disconnection. This can manifest as smugness. More commonly in readings, the Nine reversed tells a tale of narcissism: You are faced with others' inability to see beyond their own immediate needs. This influence can infect personal and professional relationships, which suffer as others forge ahead with their agendas for short-term gain, leaving you bruised. However, it's also worth asking yourself if you are the one overstriving for recognition, sidelining others in the process.

In personal and business projects, uncertainty rules due to misunderstand-ings, and your plans may be delayed. Creativity can suffer at this time, too, with stop-start-stop frustration. Focus on maintaining balance and routine to help you navigate these difficult waters and hold on to those dreams and schemes. This may not be the right time for new ideas idea to flourish, but this doesn't diminish your worth or the strength of your concepts. Take extra care of yourself and your relationships now, as energy levels may be low; hibernate a little until that spark returns.

TEN OF CUPS

KEY MEANINGS: Prosperity, joy, family, and contentment

UPRIGHT MEANING

One of the most positive cards of the minor arcana, the Ten of Cups reveals the benefits of love and the security of family; it favors children as an expression of love, and often reveals that they will do well socially and academically. The card predicts great happiness for couples, families, and close friendship groups. In work, the Ten of Cups shows peace and harmony for business partnerships and other key networks. Togetherness, not competition, is your strength. Anything you do en masse will go well, from sporting activities, committees, and choirs to group trips and collaborative projects.

In relationships, this is an emotional time, in wholly a positive way. Partnerships built on stability and trust become even more rewarding and supportive. Different generations of a family may come together and put aside old disagreements; it's a common card for forthcoming weddings, parties, and other celebrations. Communication between parents, children, grandparents, and other family members will grow stronger and be more fulfilling. If you have been searching for a new home, the Ten of Cups shows this will come to you, and it will be the right property in the right location.

In relation to projects, the card gives assurance that what you have worked hard for will finally come together. Financially, the Ten of Cups is a wonderful indicator of prosperity, which comes to you as a result of well-deserved achievement.

REVERSED MEANING

When reversed, the Ten of Cups retains much of its positive vibe, but with some irritating undercurrents and changes in friendships and family bonds. A family issue may need to be addressed as your routine is disrupted, or you sense discord in some relationships; also, you may feel that you're not getting an entitlement, from respect from different generations of the family to enjoying enough time with children. Your plans to bring friends and family together may falter due to miscommunication. Equally, the need to keep up appearances prevents authentic conversations and understanding.

Friends may also prove troublesome under the influence of the reversed Ten of Cups, and as a result, one or two confidants step back from your circle or introduce you to a new friend of theirs with whom you don't feel comfortable—which upsets your usually happy dynamic. However, other people you prefer will soon come into your orbit to take their place.

Do bear in mind, however, that these are temporary glitches, rather than major challenges—and that the reversed Ten of Cups' overriding meaning is still positive.

PAGE OF CUPS

KEY MEANINGS: Love news

UPRIGHT MEANING

AS A PERSON: An individual with an artistic temperament, this Page is a dreamer. He loves company, is highly emotional and intuitive, and is naturally generous, sometimes to a fault. He is a good friend and happy to introduce others into his circle. The Page can often indicate a sensitive child or other young person you care for.

AS THE "YOU" CARD IN A READING: It's time to enjoy life's pleasures.

AS AN INFLUENCE: The Page reresents sociability, good company, and fun. Whatever your age, the Page reveals you will feel young at heart. As Pages are messengers, the Page of Cups brings good news about the emotional aspects of your life: relationships, children, and finances (when this has a direct impact on your relationships). In love, he can show a new potential partner is coming. This is not the Page himself—he is simply the messenger—but he lets you know that love is once more on the horizon. While it will be tempting to rush into a new romance, it may be wise to hold back a little. Other responsibilities such as extra work and exams can't be abandoned just yet.

This card also favors imagination and creativity, and so augers well for new projects and opportunities to improve your home and lifestyle. If you have suffered periods of insecurity and doubt, the Page assures you that all is well and good times are ahead. Finances are also favored now.

If two or more Pages fall close together in a reading, the meanings are as follows:

> **TWO PAGES:** Friendship if upright; rivalry if one or both cards are reversed
>
> **THREE PAGES:** Lots of social activities
>
> **FOUR PAGES:** A social group of young people

REVERSED MEANING

When reversed, the Page brings frustration and irresponsibility. Offers do not materialize; you may feel that life is all work and no play. As a person, the reversed Page is emotionally immature and attention-seeking, so you cannot rely on his perspective—he can only obsess about his own needs. This person may be living in a dream world and become very defensive when challenged. In family relationships, a child may find it difficult to communicate his or her feelings.

An additional meaning of the reversed Page is intoxication—too much partying. It's time to calm down and get back to an ordered routine.

KNIGHT OF CUPS

KEY MEANINGS: A proposal

UPRIGHT MEANING

AS A PERSON: Idealistic and dreamy, artistic and sensitive, this Knight is a true romantic. His arrival in a reading shows a love prospect and even a proposal—which is wonderful if you have an established relationship. However, as a new love interest, tread carefully. This Knight is an idealist and, while wanting a relationship, finds it hard to articulate his true feelings. He may be stuck behind a persona of the perfect partner—gallant and generous—but unable to drop the act to let you see who he really is. While this is understandable in the early days of a romance, if the actions don't match the words of passion, take care; don't be swept away just yet.

AS THE "YOU" CARD IN A READING: Be open to real love; judge not by appearance.

AS AN INFLUENCE: The Knight of Cups heralds an emotional time—you may be bewitched by a new love interest (or even more than one), enjoy more romance with an existing partner, and/or other sweet things that capture your imagination: beauty, nature, time away from work or your usual routines, or creative pursuits. New friends may enter your circle.

If two or more Knights fall close together in a reading, the meanings are as follows:

> **TWO KNIGHTS:** Friendship if upright; rivalry if one or both cards are reversed
>
> **THREE KNIGHTS:** Men meeting up
>
> **FOUR KNIGHTS:** Lots of action; events speed up

REVERSED MEANING

The Knight reversed means disappointment—an offer that at first glance appeared perfect does not materialize, leaving you feeling confused and pushed out. As a person, the reversed Knight is untrustworthy and unreliable. He is hooked on the chase, the romantic or sexual ideal, but has no intention of going beyond the honeymoon phase of a relationship. He may also be looking for the thrill of new romance elsewhere, continuing the cycle of manipulation.

This card often appears in a reading to denote a lover who has intimacy and commitment issues. His behavior may be inconsistent and unpredictable, but when challenged, he may protest that this is not the case and try to deflect the problem onto you. It is of course best for you to step away, as this knight has little to offer other than ongoing drama.

QUEEN OF CUPS

KEY MEANINGS: An intuitive woman

UPRIGHT MEANING

AS A PERSON: The Queen of Cups predicts the positive influence of an intuitive, sensitive woman. She is nurturing and compassionate, with high emotional intelligence. Her work may be artistic, and she may also be drawn to medicine, caregiving, complementary therapies, certain types of sales work, or research in nonmainstream subjects. Given her sensitivity and natural empathy, this Queen has to choose her close friends carefully—but when she makes a connection with a person, she treasures him or her, just like her chalice.

This card often comes up in readings to show the ideal female partner, who is unafraid of intimacy while having stability and appropriate boundaries. It can predict motherhood and children, too.

AS THE "YOU" CARD IN A READING: Loving and giving, you make the world a better place.

AS AN INFLUENCE: Love and happiness are foremost—falling in love, loving behavior, and emotional honesty. All you need to do is follow your heart. Creative projects are favored, too. Pay attention, also, to your dreams, which hold messages for you.

If two or more Queens fall close together in a reading, the meanings are as follows:

> **TWO QUEENS:** Rivalry
>
> **THREE QUEENS:** Helpful friends
>
> **FOUR QUEENS:** Women meeting up

REVERSED MEANING

When the reversed Queen of Cups appears, you suffer emotional or financial pressure. There may be jealousy in a relationship, and most negatively, the card in this aspect can show that someone is unfaithful. As a person, the reversed Queen has obsessive tendencies, competes for attention, and needs to have her own way at all times. She drains those around her, so try not to facilitate her needs. She is not one to commit to love or contribute financially.

KING OF CUPS

KEY MEANINGS: A charismatic man

UPRIGHT MEANING

AS A PERSON: The King of Cups shows a warmhearted, charismatic male. He might be an academic, lawyer, advisor, businessman, scientist, or artist. In his work, he follows his intuition. In friendships, he is sociable, but, like his counterpart the Queen of Cups, is sensitive and needs to choose his closest friends wisely. For this reason, he may have one or two confidants and a wide circle of acquaintances. While being empathic, at times he tries to control his feelings and can come across as distant. He often needs time to process his intense emotions before sharing them.

This card often comes up in readings to show the ideal romantic partner, who is unafraid of intimacy while having stability and appropriate boundaries. It can predict fatherhood and children, too.

AS THE "YOU" CARD IN A READING: Follow your heart.

AS AN INFLUENCE: A need exists to settle a conflict, either within yourself or between you and others, usually in a work or family situation. You are unsure whether to be logical or left-field, to go with the consensus or go with a hunch. If in doubt, follow your intuition and let your heart rule. In negotiations, use all your charm and empathy. When others feel that you are really engaged with them, they will drop their defenses and communication will improve.

If two or more Kings fall close together in a reading, the meanings are as follows:

> **TWO KINGS:** A good partnership
>
> **THREE KINGS:** Influential men
>
> **FOUR KINGS:** A power battle

REVERSED MEANING

The reversed King reveals emotional vulnerability. If this applies to an individual in your life, you may be dealing with someone who is volatile right now. This person may be secretive, ashamed, and uncommunicative when not blaming others for their predicament. Thankfully, this situation is temporary and will change.

An additional meaning of the reversed card is a person with destructive behavior patterns and possibly addiction issues (see also XV, The Devil).

ACE OF PENTACLES

KEY MEANINGS: Prosperity, property, and beginnings

UPRIGHT MEANING

The upright meaning of the Ace of Pentacles is auspicious for every aspect of your life. In a spread, it overrules other minor arcana cards close by (just like XIX, The Sun). The Ace predicts happiness and contentment; you can have what you desire. Traditionally, it predicts prosperity, and you find money comes to you quickly, either as a windfall or win, or you are shown the way to achieve it. In this sense, the card presents an opportunity for further attainment, so now is the time to receive the precious gift or opportunity on offer and use it to maximize your potential. You may find a way to use it to build for the future, as property is favored in the suit of Pentacles.

In readings, it commonly arises to show money is coming or a new property; it also predicts foundation and stability, so if you have questions concerning your home or relationship, you will receive what you need in abundance. One message of the card, too, is not to doubt your good fortune. You deserve it.

In a reading, one Ace brings a focus on the life area according to the suit, which can set the theme of the reading. If two or more Aces appear near each other in a reading, it means as follows:

    TWO ACES: An important partnership

    THREE ACES: Good news

    FOUR ACES: Excitement, beginnings, and potential

REVERSED MEANING

When the Ace reverses, it reveals greed and holding fast to one outcome. This desperation can cause materialistic thinking, and when you are fixed to one goal, other aspects of your life may suffer. The card can show unwise investment of time or money, so be aware of the motives of those you invest with or work for; this can be a difficult time when you are treated unfairly by an unscrupulous person or organization. Money for work you have done may not materialize. The reversed Ace of Pentacles also shows financial mismanagement and mistakes; as a prediction card in a reading, it advises not to make major financial decisions at present.

In personal relationships, the card can show that someone close becomes grasping and materialistic and selfishly wants to keep everything for themselves. The card can also show gambling and reckless spending.

TWO OF PENTACLES

KEY MEANINGS: Negotiation

UPRIGHT MEANING

In the upright position, the card shows making a decision and in particular, managing money. There may be temporary cash-flow issues, and you'll need consistent effort to balance the books. If your income is up and down, an unexpected expenditure can hit hard; this is a common card for freelancers whose income varies from month to month, as well as for two people in business together. On a more positive note, the card says that if you pay close attention to financial and property matters, you will manage well, even on a tight budget. As a personality trait in the person/situation position in a spread, the Two of Pentacles indicates fairness and a willingness to find a good balance between work and personal life.

In readings, the card often comes up to show two properties and sometimes making a decision about where to live—in particular, a choice between home and a property abroad. This may also reveal a choice between two jobs in different places and weighing the pros and cons of each offer.

An additional meaning is news that comes in writing, so you may receive an important letter or email.

REVERSED MEANING

In the reversed position, egotism and pride can get in the way of practicality. Irresponsible spending may cause hardship, and these financial mistakes may be hidden—gambling is a common meaning here, as well as a generally reckless attitude toward money.

In work, you may be dealing with an unreasonable boss who is unrealistic about what can be achieved, putting you under needless pressure.

The card can also show the ending of a business partnership due to financial difficulties; one of you may be investing more resources into the business than the other. The message is to observe closely just how committed you and your colleagues are and if the contribution is fair and equal.

THREE OF PENTACLES

KEY MEANINGS: Enterprise and success

UPRIGHT MEANING

The upright meaning of the Three of Pentacles is rewarding work. It often shows you are ready to let your talents shine in public, and the card often appears in readings to show launching a business, receiving a commission, giving a lecture or teaching, or presiding over an important event; specifically, it can also show making a speech at a graduation or wedding, for example.

In domestic affairs, the card can predict building or improvement work to your home or putting a property up for sale. The Three of Pentacles is also a good card for creatives, predicting that projects will be finished and appreciated. The work may also be displayed in a public space.

According to tarot scholar Jonathan Dee, the Three of Pentacles is sometimes called the Architect, which means you establish a lasting enterprise, a project that "causes you to stand head and shoulders above both friends and enemies alike." The downside, of course, as you succeed and become visibly successful, is the touch of envy you may sense around you; it may feel uncomfortable, as you're not used to negative attention. This jealousy, as with elements of all minor arcana cards, is transitory and will not dint your confidence or harm your progress. Detractors can only make you stronger.

REVERSED MEANING

When the Three of Pentacles reverses, work is tiresome and you may not be willing to put in the groundwork—or to work at all. This may be because you feel you've seen it all before and have become cynical about finding a career that will suit, or you take on a role for the perceived glamour—or the way it is sold to you—and later realize that the work is mostly tedium. You'll need to push through the dull details or make a swift decision to move on.

Another interpretation of the card is poor planning so a project doesn't succeed. In property affairs, it can show builders who do not finish the work they begin.

FOUR OF PENTACLES

KEY MEANINGS: Security, self-improvement,
and holding on to money

UPRIGHT MEANING

The upright Four of Pentacles shows the need for stability and establishing a firm foundation. If you have suffered past hardship, the Four of Pentacles shows the tough times are over, as now your work pays off. While this doesn't indicate a huge windfall (look to the Ten of Pentacles for this), you will have enough money and acknowledgment to feel satisfied. The card also shows protection of assets and traditional values. Proving a strong foundation for a growing family may be important to you now, so you may consider moving to a new home or investing in a small business that will bring you future dividends. In work, you attain a position that is very secure, so if your work is temporary, for example, the Four of Pentacles can show you being offered a permanent contract.

An additional meaning of the card is the miser, as the male figure is clinging hard to his coin, but this money has come from hard work. You will value what you have achieved, and for now, want to keep it for yourself.

REVERSED MEANING

When reversed, the Four of Pentacles reveals an overly materialistic individual, a would-be king—male or female—who holds too fast to status and possessions. If this is you, try to let go of insecurity, as this can take up much of your head space—and feed an ongoing belief that you will never have enough. In work, the card can reveal that you miss opportunities because your confidence is low, and changes to your role may leave you feeling disempowered. It's therefore important to do well in any professional or educational tests now; you may need to put in more work than first anticipated.

The reversed Four of Pentacles can also suggest a person who is showy and even a little smug; in a position of power over you, you may find this individual controlling and self-centered.

FIVE OF PENTACLES

KEY MEANINGS: A test of resources

UPRIGHT MEANING

The traditional meaning of the Five of Pentacles is financial loss, so when it shows up in a reading, it can mean losing a job or a relationship or experiencing some other financial or emotional hardship. The positive aspect is that you find support from others in a similar position. These contacts may become good friends whom you may never have met in your usual circumstances. Consider new options, and you may discover another resource or approach that will help you see a way forward.

However, this card often comes up in readings to show a fear of poverty and isolation, rather than actual poverty. It also commonly shows a fear of losing the security of home and/or the aftermath of a relationship breakup, with one partner feeling alone and depleted. It occasionally reveals the impact of bereavement. While tarot cards do not predict death, the Five of Pentacles when in the present/situation position in a reading (rather than the future position) can reflect the feelings of sadness as a result of losing someone close.

REVERSED MEANING

There's a moral theme to the interpretation for the reversed Five of Pentacles, in that the card asks you to examine your values. If you're clinging to objects, people, or money, what are you avoiding? Fear of change could lead you to ignore debt or become oblivious to growing tension in a relationship. Hoarding old possessions and memories shows you need to feel safe for now and don't have the confidence or the faith that you will be supported in the future—at least, just at present. As with all minor arcana cards, though, this is a temporary influence.

In relationships, you may suffer due to a partner's selfish behavior. This person doesn't want to give to you emotionally, or he or she withholds money. The card can also show you being ill-treated by an ex-partner who doesn't pay what is due.

SIX OF PENTACLES

KEY MEANINGS: Property, family, inheritance

UPRIGHT MEANING

The upright card shows that money is coming to you. It may arrive as a gift or an award and may be donated by an individual rather than an organization. This allows you to pay off any outstanding debt and/or invest the money wisely in your future. If you have been struggling financially, this card is a welcome sign that your circumstances will certainly improve. Equally, the card can show that you are the benefactor, so you may help a friend in need with a temporary cash-flow problem, or you feel drawn to support a charity that is close to your heart. Whomever you choose to help, you will consider carefully his or her needs and offer the right amount to make a difference.

Overall, this card brings genuine support and predicts you feeling connected and close to your usual circle of friends and family. Together, you may be exchanging small gifts of appreciation.

An additional meaning is receiving help or money from a person from your past or using savings to help another person.

REVERSED MEANING

When reversed, the Six of Pentacles shows money coming to you but you cannot keep it—usually due to carelessness or theft. A traditional meaning of the card is having your purse or wallet stolen, and this message is reinforced if the reversed card is placed close to the Seven of Swords, the "thief" card of the minor arcana. Guard your possessions carefully and watch what you spend so that enough money stays in your pocket. The reversed card also suggests there may be envy due to money, so monitor your attitudes and the attitudes of people around you.

An alternative interpretation is an offer of money, but it comes with conditions that are not acceptable to you. The message here is not to compromise and to say no if you need to. There will be other options.

SEVEN OF PENTACLES

KEY MEANINGS: Work and the potential for success

UPRIGHT MEANING

There's a goal in sight, and you are close to achieving it—but now is not the time to stop and reflect. The Seven of Pentacles is the card of doing, not philosophizing, so keep your focus on what you want and believe you can achieve it. This effort may feel relentless, but your hard work will pay off.

The card often comes up in readings to show the need to keep the focus on your career goals or to work through a particularly tedious stage in a current project that leaves you feeling tired and deflated. You might be tired of the relentlessness of it all, but the reward will come as long as you don't falter. Also, the Seven can show saving for a home or accruing funds and clients to expand a business. In domestic affairs, the Seven of Pentacles can show there's not enough money left for the little luxuries that make all the effort of saving worthwhile. Whatever your situation, keep going—you are nearly there, and in the future, you will thank yourself for your dedication.

REVERSED MEANING

When reversed, the Seven of Pentacles means procrastination. Time is running out, so commit fully to the work you're doing or the lifestyle you have, regardless of the ups and downs—or put your energies elsewhere. This may mean considering a different job or career path. You may have become disheartened with slow—or no—progress in your work or improvement in your finances, but while you're in the doldrums, opportunities can slip away. Muster your willpower and take action now: Any decision is better than no decision at all.

An additional meaning of the card is anxiety about a loan or other financial agreement. If this is affecting your motivation, try to renegotiate terms, rather than give up now.

EIGHT OF PENTACLES

KEY MEANINGS: Education and achievement

UPRIGHT MEANING

Money is on its way, often as a result of previous efforts or decisions rather than an unexpected bonus or gift. (Look to the Six or Ten of Pentacles for generosity and windfalls.) You may be offered an opportunity to gain new skills that will be profitable in the long term. You may also consider a new career direction or be working for promotion. In general, the card also reflects the need for a logical, diligent approach to your projects.

This card is often known as the apprentice. It comes up in readings to show education and gaining a qualification, particularly an undergraduate degree or diploma. The Eight of Pentacles also shows a personality aspect, so if it appears in the "you/situation" position in a spread, it reveals a hardworking, trustworthy, and dedicated individual who takes his or her responsibilities seriously.

REVERSED MEANING

The reversed Eight of Pentacles can show that you're feeling trapped. This may be because you've chosen an educational course that isn't for you and doesn't develop your particular talents or reflect your interests enough to be sustainable long term. In work, you may know you're only doing the job for the money. While this may be acceptable on a short-term basis, long term it feels soul-destroying. While supporting yourself financially, it may be time to look elsewhere rather than let the situation continue.

As a prediction card, the Eight of Pentacles shows a cycle is about to come to an end, so rather than wait for this to happen, conserve your energy and direct it toward finding a new career. Don't resign yourself to your present situation if there's no sense of achievement or appreciation.

NINE OF PENTACLES

KEY MEANINGS: Comfort, accomplishment, and prosperity

UPRIGHT MEANING

The Nine ushers in a time of financial stability. You can feel safe in your home and proud of your achievements. At last, you can surround yourself with the material objects you love, and you may find yourself redecorating your home or tending your garden or yard. It's time to appreciate all that you have, so leisure time beckons; treat yourself to whatever makes you happy and enjoy the fruits of your work. You will be able to focus on your own needs without feeling guilty. The Nine also brings a sense of serenity and relaxation, so the card predicts you can feel at home and at one with yourself.

This card often comes up in a reading to show a woman of independent means who is generous and well balanced. In this way, the Nine of Pentacles is similar to the Queen of Pentacles, although the Queen's influence is generally greater. In work matters, the card can predict financial reward, such as a bonus, for your efforts.

REVERSED MEANING

When reversed, the card can show vanity and ego at large—the urge for material wealth gets out of control, so overspending (or dealing with a loved one's overspending) may need to be confronted. In general, the card can show financial dependence that is uncomfortable or misuse of money for selfish means.

An additional meaning is feeling that your home is somehow under threat because you are struggling with debt. Don't struggle alone—help is at hand.

TEN OF PENTACLES

KEY MEANINGS: Property, family, and inheritance

UPRIGHT MEANING

The upright Ten of Pentacles shows an inheritance, generosity, and a love relationship that brings wealth and happiness—so if you are asking the question, "Will my current relationship get more committed?" the answer will be a resounding yes. The Ten of Pentacles often comes up in readings to show a wedding. What is even better is that the couple shares similar values and often has similar cultural backgrounds (and the two families actually like one another!).

An additional meaning is inherited property, buying a second home, or extending your current home, again with family support. At this time, you also benefit from sharing—your time, resources, skills, or money to help each other out. Note that family in this context signifies those you consider family and treat as such, so this could relate to a close circle of longtime friends.

This card also suggests maturity. You can interpret this in financial terms, with investments maturing, as well as in emotional terms, as the emotional maturity that comes with life experience. You may find that an older person in the family has wisdom to share in addition to resources.

REVERSED MEANING

When reversed, the Ten of Pentacles reveals communication problems in families as one generation tries to dominate another; children and parents disagree and have very different attitudes. The card can highlight contention over a specific issue, such as conflict over property or money. Equally, general attitudes toward finances may be at the heart of the problem. This card often comes up in readings to show overly strict parents who try to control their families with money.

There is also an issue with status here as traditional values block freedom of expression. Older people may find it hard to accept that their children want to do things differently.

In romantic relationships, money, property issues, and the demands of family get in the way of love. Ambition takes over; personal life comes second.

PAGE OF PENTACLES

KEY MEANINGS: Talent shines and money news

UPRIGHT MEANING

AS A PERSON: Hardworking and methodical, reliable and dedicated—this Page is practical and trustworthy. As a Page, he is a younger person, or someone with youthful vigor. He may be starting out in the world, or in a new line of business. He may not have money now, but he has the potential to achieve great things, so believe in him and his plans; he will not give up.

The card can also show a young person's achievement and reward for his or her efforts in sport or education.

AS THE "YOU" CARD IN A READING: Money and opportunities beckon— you have an opportunity to establish a new venture.

AS AN INFLUENCE: This Page reveals progress and adventure, as well as auspicious beginnings. This is a time to nurture your skills and abilities. There will be good news concerning finances, business, education, and travel. The Page of Pentacles also highlights the need for management; there may be an opportunity to manage people and projects at work. This Page often appears to show a job offer or an offer made on a property.

THE CARD DOES COME WITH AN ELEMENT OF CAUTION, HOWEVER: There is a real need for attention to detail now and for diligence in all practical affairs, so double-check all arrangements and agreements. Also, check your personal schedule to ensure everything you plan is realistic. The Page can also be a sign to attend to finances; he comes up in readings to nudge us to do our taxes and renew outstanding insurance policies.

See page 83 for meanings if two or more Pages fall close together in a reading.

REVERSED MEANING

When the Page of Pentacles is reversed, there may be unwelcome news regarding finances or property. Unlike the responsible upright Page, the card in this position means extravagance and irresponsibility rule. You may suffer due to someone else's selfish actions. This may apply to young people you live with or to friends with immature tendencies.

The card can also apply to a person with a sense of entitlement who helps himself to what is yours; while this is not necessarily theft, it is underhanded. Observe and take note for future reference.

KNIGHT OF PENTACLES

KEY MEANINGS: Improving prosperity

UPRIGHT MEANING

AS A PERSON: This Knight is loyal and dependable. He is a natural protector, and security is very important to him. He may work in property or finance.

As a potential partner, he has much to offer and is genuine. For some, he may lack excitement, as he plans rather than reacts; he can be slow to judge and to express his feelings, and keeps on safe subjects. Depending on what you need from a relationship, he could be a gift—your rock through thick and thin. If you crave excitement, he won't be entertaining enough to capture your heart.

AS THE "YOU" CARD IN A READING: Invest your time wisely. Be consistent in your efforts.

AS AN INFLUENCE: Showing financial growth and good investment, this card means plans concerning property progress. With strategizing and setting a realistic goal, you will succeed. Pay attention to the practical details now, and future benefits are assured. Day to day, this Knight asks you to get through boring and routine, but essential, tasks. In work, the card can indicate more money coming to you due to a raise, bonus, or promotion, but you may need to work harder in return.

An additional meaning of the card is finding a secure home, potentially with a partner.

See page 85 for meanings if two or more Knights fall close together in a reading.

REVERSED MEANING

When reversed, the card advises that you avoid complacency and check out all financial arrangements. The most negative interpretation of the card is financial mismanagement and misleading advice.

As a person, the reversed Knight is stubborn and cannot see others' viewpoints. He is plodding and pessimistic, reluctant to take action and unwilling to go beyond his comfort zone. He may tend to be materialistic and secretive and, in extremis, dishonest.

QUEEN OF PENTACLES

KEY MEANINGS: A reliable woman

UPRIGHT MEANING

AS A PERSON: The Queen of Pentacles is usually well off, generous, and supportive. She has a strong maternal instinct, is affectionate and wise—and she may be an older woman, or a younger female with wisdom beyond her years.

Her vocations include public office, ecology, agriculture, politics, sports coaching, food and catering, and business—any work that benefits large numbers of people. She may be a homemaker, as she loves caring for her home and garden. She likes the good things in life and knows how to spend money well—on beautiful objects, on gifts for loved ones, and of course, on herself. She is physically affectionate and hands-on in her projects; rather than dictating from the sidelines, she will lend practical help.

In readings, she commonly shows up as a benefactor.

AS THE "YOU" CARD IN A READING: Care for your body and your finances.

AS AN INFLUENCE: In addition to practical support, wisdom, good financial management, and financial help, the Queen of Pentacles can show marriage and money coming to a couple. It is also a positive card for good health, a sensual sex life, fertility, and children.

See page 87 for meanings if two or more Queens fall close together in a reading.

REVERSED MEANING

When this card is reversed, finances can suffer. Money you relied upon doesn't roll in or funds are misappropriated. You may have to deal with the impact of someone's financial mishaps. This is temporary, however. An additional meaning is your home is neglected while other concerns take over.

As a person, the reversed Queen can be stubborn and unimaginative. She can be mean with money, or at the other extreme, an emotional spender. Her erratic behavior is for self-comfort, or she uses money to buy other people's affection.

KING OF PENTACLES

KEY MEANINGS: A generous man

UPRIGHT MEANING

AS A PERSON: A visionary man with a plan, the King will work hard for rewards and is usually well off. He is reliable and generous and offers practical support. Security is important to him, and he is happiest in a settled relationship. He needs to be a protector, and he has firm boundaries—he will not tolerate those looking to take what is his. His ideal vocations include property and building, business, accounting or any work that is number-based, as well as agriculture or land management. An additional meaning is a generous benefactor.

AS THE "YOU" CARD IN A READING: Make the most of your assets.

AS AN INFLUENCE: Financial and property matters improve, and you enjoy success and comfort. The King of Pentacles also predicts conflicts that will be resolved. In relationships, he offers security and loyalty.

See page 89 for meanings if two or more Kings fall close together in a reading.

REVERSED MEANING

When reversed, the King is greedy and untrustworthy, so double-check all financial agreements to ensure that there are no hidden catches. Debt is an interpretation of the reversed King, so turn the spotlight on your finances now to limit the damage of overspending.

As a person, the reversed King is corrupt and may be involved in fraud or gambling. He is determined to win at any cost.

ACE OF SWORDS

KEY MEANINGS: Success, decisions, and beginnings

UPRIGHT MEANING

The upright meaning of the Ace is auspicious for every aspect of your life. In a spread, it overrules any negative minor arcana cards close by (just like the major arcana card XIX, The Sun). The Ace of Swords predicts new beginnings, decisions, and clear thinking and usually relates to work and love. It heralds action, drama, and sometimes confrontation. However the Ace of Swords manifests in your life, it will bring an immediate change to your circumstances—for the better.

As a prediction card, it shows that mental agility and assertiveness will bring success. The other cards around the Ace in a reading will guide you to the nature of this conquest. Be cautious, though, not to be too zealous—judge the situation and be direct, rather than abrasive, mindful of how you would want to be treated if you were on the receiving end.

In relationships, it reveals triumph over past obstacles—you win through to your heart's desire.

In a reading, one Ace brings a focus on the life area according to the suit, which can set the theme of the reading. If two or more Aces appear near each other in a reading, it means the following:

TWO ACES: An important partnership

THREE ACES: Good news

FOUR ACES: Excitement, beginnings, and potential

REVERSED MEANING

When the Ace reverses, the card can predict conflict and arguments, and you may become involved in a hurtful battle of wills. The card can also predict a contest that you cannot win, at least at present. The message is to withdraw, tend your wounds, and turn your attentions elsewhere.

You may also lack confidence in your intellectual abilities just now and not feel equal to others—which is your perception, not the reality.

Another common meaning of the reversed Ace in readings is a decision going against you, such as failing a test or interview and, in more general terms, not being able to hold your ground under fire from more dominant personalities.

TWO OF SWORDS

KEY MEANINGS: Time to think and a stalemate

UPRIGHT MEANING

The Two of Swords shows thinking time before a decision. A situation has reached a stalemate, so you can view this period as a truce or a rest before further negotiation. The tendency is to protect yourself, have a little peace, and not take action. Unfortunately, this upcoming battle may not go away; resolve it now and it's done. Otherwise, the situation festers and may return. As there are two swords on the card, this Two can reveal a person you cross swords with. It's likely that your difficult person is sharp-tongued, but don't be afraid of a lashing: Stand your ground and say what you think.

The card commonly comes up in readings to show employment issues and also time out in relationships. This may be circumstantial, due to partners living in different places; if negative cards such as the Three of Swords or Lovers reversed appears with the Two of Swords, it shows making a decision about the future of a relationship.

Whatever your experience of the Two of Swords, help is at hand in the form of supportive friends and colleagues. Listen to advice and then take the best practical steps forward.

REVERSED MEANING

When reversed, the traditional meaning of the Two of Swords is deception and being blind to someone's manipulation. This card applies particularly to partnerships—love, friendships, and in business and your career. If your intuition is telling you that someone is dishonest, pay attention and carry out your own detailed investigation to get to the heart of the matter. There is an opportunity here to act, but the timing is sensitive; the message is not to delay.

THREE OF SWORDS

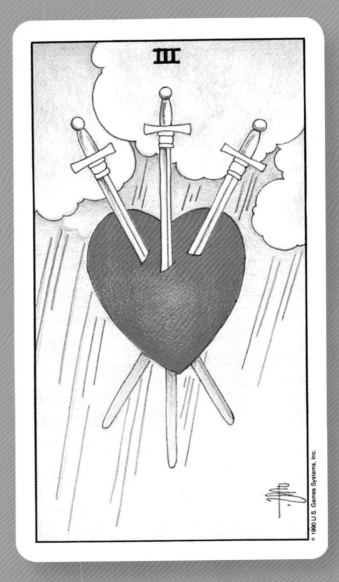

KEY MEANINGS: Sorrow, heartbreak, and pain

UPRIGHT MEANING

The upright Three of Swords is direct in its meaning and reveals the pain of truth. The clouds of doubt are cleared, and you can do nothing but face reality. This is a common card for relationship betrayal and can denote affairs or disloyalty in other life areas, such as work relationships and business dealings. On a more positive note, you do get right to the heart of the matter—any confusion is banished, and you are now in a position to begin to move on from shock, to begin the healing process and move forward.

In health, this Three can relate to heart issues that may need attention—such as blood pressure issues, circulatory problems, conditions such as angina, and very occasionally, the need for surgery. Please note that this is a message to take care of the heart and safeguard health; it is not a prediction of serious illness.

REVERSED MEANING

When the Three of Swords reverses, the upset of the upright card is accompanied by quarrels and drama. In a sense, despite the upheaval, this gives a more positive meaning than that of the upright card, as at least feelings are expressed and some of the confusion and pain is shared and released. Those around you will understand your need to vent.

FOUR OF SWORDS

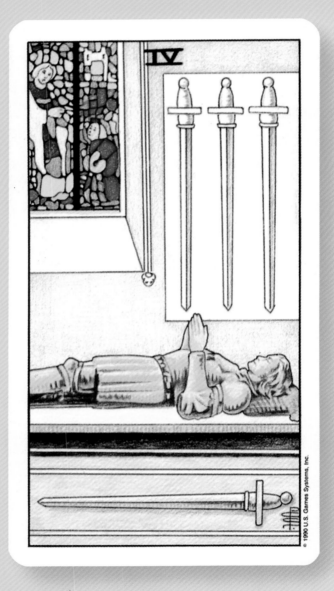

KEY MEANINGS: Rest, passivity, and quiet time

UPRIGHT MEANING

The Four of Swords has the meaning of time out, so you may be taking a rest from work, a personal project, or a relationship. The card often comes up in readings in the past or present position to show taking a break from a relationship and also the need for recovery from illness or an operation. Commonly, as a prediction card, the Four of Swords shows recovery from stress, so the message is to conserve your energy and take quiet time if you can.

The solitude of the Four of Swords can also apply to meditators and lightworkers and any individual following a spiritual path. You may need more mental space and private time than usual, so in this sense, the card is a nudge to take some alone time to recharge.

An additional meaning of the card is counseling or therapy and, rarely, attending a memorial service.

REVERSED MEANING

When the Four of Swords reverses, the time-out message is enforced— so you may have to take time away from work or other responsibilities due to influences out of your control. Unfortunately, there is little you can do to alter this situation, so you must surrender to events. This is a phase, and the message is to find peace. Use the time positively. You may need to rethink your working arrangements or come to terms with changes in a relationship, particularly if you live apart from a partner or potential love.

FIVE OF SWORDS

KEY MEANINGS: Upheaval, conflict, and loss

UPRIGHT MEANING

The traditional meaning of this Five of Swords is battle and loss. It often shows family disputes, conflicts with managers, and also being the victim of "the system"—specifically, educational boards and government and educational bodies. In relationships, the card predicts tension and conflict. Overall, the Five of Swords reveals ongoing stress, continual challenges to your position—and, often, defeat.

However this disruptive Five of Swords manifests for you, the overriding message is that all is not lost. You may not win the battle, but you can recover and walk away with your self-respect—provided you make a gracious exit at the right time. There's a danger here that you continue the fight even when the battle is over. Regardless of the provocation, deal with your anger and disappointment. There's a saying, "It's all over, bar the shouting." Don't keep shouting too much longer or hope to revisit the situation or relationship. It's done.

REVERSED MEANING

The Five of Swords reversed shows unnecessary conflict; you could become caught in the middle of another person's fight, and you may be the injured party through no fault of your own. This battle is not for good reason. Whoever initiates it has a selfish agenda; this person may be trying to cover up his or her incompetence at work, blaming others to deflect attention; equally, the drama may be due to ego and a need to make a show of power. In this sense, it can be easier to extricate yourself because you know the battle is less personal.

An additional meaning of the card is bullying and oppression. There is no shame in this—rather, the card suggests finding an opportunity to expose the unfairness and to shift the balance of power.

SIX OF SWORDS

KEY MEANINGS: Moving on

UPRIGHT MEANING

The Six of Swords shows you moving on from a situation or relationship and enjoying a period of peace and harmony. This may manifest mentally rather than physically, as you take a more detached approach, distancing yourself from drama and complication. This gives you an opportunity to rest and recharge; it may lead you to explore a new environment or make a spiritual discovery.

In work, the card can show travel as part of your role (and respite from the office or other workplace), and in relationships, the card commonly shows two people spending time apart. More negatively, the interpretation is a relationship ending (look for accompanying cards such as the Three of Swords or the revised VI, The Lovers, for validation). This ending may be positive or negative, depending on your situation.

On a more literal note, the card can simply show taking a break from work or your usual environment, and you may travel, possibly on a trip overseas. When the Six of Swords appears with major arcana cards VII, The Chariot, for progress and XIII, Death, for transition, a more permanent move is suggested, so the combination can be interpreted as emigration or a long period of travel. If we see the three figures on the card as a family rather than ferryman and passengers, the card suggests a major move for two or more people.

REVERSED MEANING

When reversed, the Six of Swords has a meaning that is similar to that of the upright card. It reveals a need to escape, but your plans are delayed. It may not be the right time for you to travel or leave an unsatisfying situation, as certain problems need to be addressed and resolved before you can be free. However, check that your intentions are sound and that you're looking in the right direction; rather than fixating on a particular outcome, which may blind you to other possibilities, keep your plans realistic. You may feel frustrated now by lack of progress, but stay focused and grounded and your time will come.

SEVEN OF SWORDS

KEY MEANINGS: Theft and dishonesty

UPRIGHT MEANING

The common name for this Seven of Swords is "the thief." Traditionally, the message is to protect your belongings and property. In general, we can think of this as a potential transgression—you may encounter a challenge to your position, an individual invading your space, or in relationships, a selfish partner who takes too much emotionally, or at worst, defrauds you. As the suit of Swords relates to intellect, you'll need your instincts and your wits to discover the truth. You may need to be devious and play this person at his or her own game, too, to find out what you need to know. Your opponent may be strong, but you still have valuable resources on your side.

The card can also show legal problems, and unfair or fraudulent business dealings.

REVERSED MEANING

The reversed Seven of Swords shows a tendency to give up rather than take a stand. It may feel unnatural to you to think like your opponent to anticipate their next moves, but this attitude will help you defend what is yours. Otherwise, you may surrender too soon. This particularly applies to work, when a colleague tries to disempower you. It's important to stand your ground.

As with the upright card, the reversed Seven of Swords can show legal problems of and in business dealings; beware of unscrupulous people.

EIGHT OF SWORDS

KEY MEANINGS: Restriction

UPRIGHT MEANING

The upright card shows feeling trapped. This may be due to a series of bad experiences and poor luck, and you begin to wonder if things can ever improve. You may be anxious due to an unsatisfactory bond with an individual or an organization; specifically, you may be trapped by a credit agreement that leaves you little money for yourself.

This unfortunate Eight of Swords commonly reveals problems in careers and the intellectual or mental realm, showing frustration and, at its most exteme, panic. Hemmed in and unhappy, you may be finding it impossible to do your work to your satisfaction due to unreasonable demands or disorganized management. Also, there may be a sense of conversations going on behind closed doors that you are not party to, so you feel isolated and even vulnerable. The card commonly arises in readings to show someone who is in a role that doesn't suit them, but they are under pressure to conform—such as working in the family business or taking a course because it will lead to a profession, although it isn't what they love doing at all. Many creatives and lightworkers go through this experience of not fitting in, but it takes time and confidence to find your path. You can release yourself from these bonds, but it will take determination, and you may need to swallow your pride and ask others for support and advice. On a social level, the Eight of Swords can show you feeling humiliated or ignored, and you fear others' attitudes toward you.

An additional meaning of the card is illness and incapacity. Again, this does not imply permanent disability, but a phase of physical restriction.

REVERSED MEANING

In the reversed position, much of the upright meaning applies, except that it is often accompanied by strong emotions such as guilt, anger, and regret. It's likely you'll express these feelings in negative ways, however, because you are so frustrated; try not to lash out on whoever is closest. As with all the minor arcana cards, the Eight of Swords shows a phase that will not last.

NINE OF SWORDS

KEY MEANINGS: Anxiety

UPRIGHT MEANING

I call this Nine "the 3 a.m. card" because it describes the meaning so accurately: It's what you wake up worrying about in the small hours of the night, showing you are dealing with high levels of anxiety. You may have suffered an illness and the resulting low energy or a shock or a buildup of minor stresses that begin to disrupt your sleep patterns and peace of mind. External events such as these may have triggered the initial stress, but the issue now is how you are responding to it.

Look to the surrounding cards to see the life area that this relates to, although the anxiety in the Nine of Swords can reflect unhappiness in key areas, from work to relationships, coloring your usually positive attitude. The card also indicates the habit of worry—so you may be worrying about inconsequential things that usually don't warrant your attention. Thankfully, as this is a minor card, this pattern is temporary.

In work, the Nine of Swords can show feeling overwhelmed. You simply have too much to do, particularly if the card appears with the Ten of Wands, known as the burden card.

The Nine of Swords occasionally comes up in a reading to show mental health issues associated with anxiety, such as panic disorder or anxiety and depression. Insomnia and nightmares are additional interpretations.

REVERSED MEANING

Unfortunately, as you might expect, the reversed Nine's meaning is more extreme than that of its upright counterpart and traditionally means despair, guilt, or feeling trapped. However, this is the lowest point of the cycle, and these feeling will begin to shift. As you gradually move out of this difficult phase, you will feel more able to turn these feelings of powerlessness around. Be patient and compassionate with yourself and turn to others for support rather than suffering alone.

TEN OF SWORDS

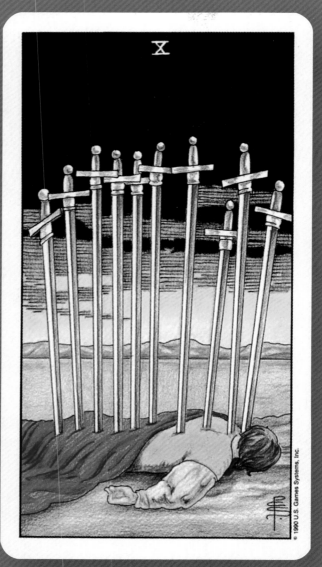

KEY MEANINGS: Endings

UPRIGHT MEANING

The traditional meaning of the upright card is ruin. While this sounds frightening, it does not, however, mean death or destruction; it is also worth bearing in mind that this event, although sudden, has a history. This is not an act of God, like the lightning strike of card XVI, The Tower, but the natural outcome of a culmination of events that leads to inevitable change. This ending clears the way for new possibilities, and you may find the finality of it releases you from frustration and stress, as is expressed in the preceding card, the Nine of Swords. In this sense, the Ten of Swords is an aspect of card XIII, Death, in its meaning of endings, transition, and new beginnings.

In your personal life, bonds of friendship may break, and there may be no turning back; this, unfortunately, is unavoidable, but with hindsight, you may see that certain people in a group were causing discord and stress. In love relationships, the card signifies a dramatic ending (particularly if it appears close to the Three of Swords, the "sorrow" card). However, the Ten of Swords often applies to a group of people, rather than individuals. In work, this may manifest as the closure of a department accompanied by job loss or a failing business.

On a more positive note, this is the end of an era; soon the strife and upset will be over. Health issues, such as low energy and exhaustion, will improve.

REVERSED MEANING

When reversed, the Ten of Swords holds the meaning of the upright card, but indicates there may be more repercussions. You may examine your past actions and feel guilty or angry and react more deeply to the fallout; try not to hold on to the stress. Accept the situation and let go.

The reversed Ten of Swords can also show feeling helpless, particularly if you have been ill or overwhelmed emotionally. Soon you will feel able to pick yourself up and start over.

PAGE OF SWORDS

KEY MEANINGS: Intelligence and contracts

UPRIGHT MEANING

AS A PERSON: The Page of Swords suggests an individual who is charming, clever, and very good company. As he's a Page, this is often a younger person or someone with a youthful, quick-fire brain. He may be forthright with his words, but he is ultimately a good ally who can turn challenges into opportunities. Quick to learn, he is curious and open, but the downside is that he can be mischievous and so set on achieving his aims he forgets to treat others with sensitivity.

AS THE "YOU" CARD IN A READING: Rely on your intelligence.

AS AN INFLUENCE: This card denotes useful information. Your hard work pays off in business and other work dealings. The Page of Swords also suggests people around you will be helpful, furthering your ambitions. This is a time to be alert and observe carefully what others say. Be ready to take action as you see the right opportunity and consult others who can act as advocates on your behalf.

This card often comes up in readings to say that a contract will be coming your way—regarding property, careers, travel documents, and other agreements.

See page 83 for meanings if two or more Pages fall close together in a reading.

REVERSED MEANING

When reversed, this clever Page of Swords becomes manipulative and cunning. Be cautious about information you receive now, as it may not be reliable, and be discerning about what you hear about other people, as it may be unjust and even slanderous. As a person, the reversed Page of Swords can be a gossip who seems to care little about the misconceptions he spreads. At his worst, he can be devious and unscrupulous. Ignore his needs for constant attention; don't fuel his fire.

KNIGHT OF SWORDS

© 1990 U.S. Games Systems, Inc.

KEY MEANINGS: Stress and truth

UPRIGHT MEANING

AS A PERSON: The Knight of Swords is determined and driven, and he has a strong sense of himself and his mission. He may be quirky and entertaining with an offbeat sense of humor, and he may even dress in a distinctive way. Incisive, forthright, and intelligent, he makes a strong advocate and is prepared to fight for his beliefs. The downside is that he often makes his mark, gets bored, and moves on. In relationships, he may cause drama, but takes no responsibility for reconciliation, leaving others to make peace while he's charging ahead with his next obsession. In work, he can show up in readings to represent auditors and other assessors, such as doctors and lawyers, or consultants who are hired to fire, not fix—in short, professionals who are adept at diagnoses and whose opinions matter. Ultimately, though, you are the one who will have to deal with the outcomes.

AS THE "YOU" CARD IN A READING: Expect the unexpected.

AS AN INFLUENCE: Unpredictable, tempestuous times are ahead—you're in for a roller coaster drama of highs and lows. Sudden truths may come to light or underlying conflicts are exposed. This may be illuminating, stressful, or bewildering, depending on your position.

The card often comes up to show disputes at work and tension within families and in romantic relationships. While you may not be responsible for the cause of the trouble, what counts now is how you recover. There is a way forward, but you may need to wait until the situation is calmer before you can make a move.

See page 85 for meanings if two or more Knights fall close together in a reading.

REVERSED MEANING

When reversed, the Knight of Swords means stressful situations are blown out of proportion as an individual thrives on drama but lacks the courage to take control. The card also advises that you may be let down by someone you thought was reliable and steadfast. A person with a big personality may have lots to say but have little substance. However, this individual's high intelligence means he usually talks his way out of trouble, denying any involvement.

QUEEN OF SWORDS

KEY MEANINGS: An incisive woman

UPRIGHT MEANING

AS A PERSON: An astute strategist, the Queen of Swords is single-minded and highly ambitious. Like her sign of Libra, she can quickly assess all aspects of a situation to get to the truth, including the underlying psychological motivation for others' attitudes and actions. Adept at numbers, she may be an administrator, IT specialist, researcher, or financial executive—the need for attention to detail relates to her associated sign of Virgo. Sword Queens also make successful businesswomen or bosses. She has much life experience and may have had hurdles to overcome in her early years. This makes her the strong woman she is. For all this, she is still willing to take risks on new experiences and relationships. She does not suffer fools gladly, but if she likes you, she will reward and trust you implicitly.

Traditionally, this card is known as the widow, but means in general a single woman or a woman who has to make her own way in the world. It's also a common card for single parents.

AS THE "YOU" CARD IN A READING: Be determined and stand strong.

AS AN INFLUENCE: The Queen of Swords offers wisdom and intelligence, perspective, and the ability to see the bigger picture. When placed close to negative cards in a reading, the Queen shows strength in adversity.

See page 87 for meanings if two or more Queens fall close together in a reading.

REVERSED MEANING

Reversed, the Queen of Swords suggests excuses for bad behavior or a situation in which you are unjustly attacked. As a person, this individual can be an opponent or someone who has suddenly turned bitter and vengeful. However, a common reason for the Queen to invert can be extreme stress—this woman lacks awareness of just how unreasonable her demands have become. If this is the case, back away; she must help herself.

KING OF SWORDS

KEY MEANINGS: An ambitious man

UPRIGHT MEANING

AS A PERSON: The King of Swords can be an intellectual or a man who relies on logic to help him win. He is also open to ideas, although he can be impatient if he has to wait for a consensus before taking action. However, he is outwardly calm and makes good judgments. He often has a dry sense of humor and is very charming. In readings, he can appear as a seductive man you meet at work or through other professional connections.

His ideal vocations include traditional professions, and you will often find him in powerful roles: doctor, judge, solicitor, or member of the armed forces or law enforcement; academic, IT, and research work may appeal, and in business, he is often a manager or director. Whatever profession he chooses, he must be able to make decisions that make a difference, and preferably, have hands-on involvement.

AS THE "YOU" CARD IN A READING: Take charge.

AS AN INFLUENCE: When the King of Swords arrives in a reading, the focus is on the mind rather than the heart. You may be going through an intensive time of work or study. In relationships and domestic affairs, it's time to take the initiative.

See page 89 for meanings if two or more Kings fall close together in a reading.

REVERSED MEANING

When reversed, the influence of the usually balanced King of Swords can be destructive. You may be put under unreasonable pressure to produce results. Unfortunately, there's no room for argument or personal interpretations, so you may feel oppressed. Thankfully, this is a temporary situation. As a person, you may be dealing with someone who plays mind games and who will do almost anything to win.

ACE OF WANDS

KEY MEANINGS: Enterprise, career, travel, and beginnings

UPRIGHT MEANING

The upright meaning of the Ace of Wands is auspicious for every aspect of your life. In a spread, it overrules any negative minor arcana cards close by (just like the major arcana card XIX, The Sun). The Ace predicts new beginnings, enterprise, and invention and often relates to work issues and projects. It's a happy card for creative work, too. With this Ace, you experience a flash of inspiration and know what do next to give form to your concept.

You conceive ideas, so the card works at a literal level as a phallic symbol, for male virility and starting a family.

An additional meaning of the card is travel and adventure, particularly when it appears in a reading with the Three or Eight of Wands.

In a reading, one Ace brings a focus on the life area according to the suit, which can set the theme of the reading. If two or more Aces appear near each other in a reading, it means the following:

TWO ACES: An important partnership

THREE ACES: Good news

FOUR ACES: Excitement, beginnings, and potential

REVERSED MEANING

When the Ace of Wands reverses, it can show blocks to creative projects and delays to travel. In work, a project may be abandoned or postponed due to poor management. In general, the card reveals false starts; plans need to be rethought.

In relationships, this Ace can reveal a lack of commitment from a man or time apart for a couple, usually due to work, and the woman finds herself waiting for the man.

Another common meaning of the reversed Ace of Wands in readings is difficulty conceiving a child, particularly if the card appears close to the Three of Swords, the card for sorrow.

TWO OF WANDS

KEY MEANINGS: Plans, partnership, and influence

UPRIGHT MEANING

The Two of Wands shows you making plans and moving forward, so travel arrangements are one meaning of the card. In your work, you are gaining influence and proving your worth. In return, you receive good support and advice. The card can also show new creative partnerships and beginning a new project or enterprise.

As there are two wands on the card, there are also two aspects to your situation. Consider what helps you on your path and any issues that hold you back. Make a plan that maximizes your strengths so your talent continues to shine.

An additional meaning of the Two of Wands is a new romantic partnership, and it often comes up in a reading to reveal that the relationship begins at work or through a mutual friendship or leisure interests. Spiritually, too, you are feeling more connected within yourself and the world at large, so you may feel drawn to development courses or simply spending time connecting with nature.

Overall, great opportunities are on the way, allowing you to move up a level. Make the most of these offers—your star is rising.

REVERSED MEANING

When reversed, your talent may be wasted because those who can help you progress are not listening. If this is the case, consider a change of scenery. You need to be with people who understand your views and appreciate your skills. The card can also show misplaced trust and an unreliable partner. Check if those close to you are pulling their weight—or you could be the one doing all the work. In relationships, a partner is unreliable.

THREE OF WANDS

KEY MEANINGS: Action and adventure

UPRIGHT MEANING

The Three of Wands is one of the tarot's good-fortune cards. It reveals successful enterprise and seeing your projects and relationships thrive; it is also a great indicator for weddings and a new, important relationship. It predicts a busy, intense period of activity—so be prepared to be inundated with texts, emails, calls, and visitors.

This card is often an indicator of an imminent trip away and seeing your plans realized—whether those are travel plans, business plans, a wedding, or other projects you have nurtured. This is also a time for great communication and self-expression through chosen interests such as art, music, crafts, and sport. The Three of Wands also favors individuality and nonconformism, so you may feel drawn to unconventional people and projects now. Also, pride yourself on your quirks and eccentricities, and let others see all you have to offer rather than the aspects of you with which you assume they are most comfortable. From this, you can gain even more confidence and even admiration. You are unique, after all.

The Three's challenge is to keep the balance between staying focused on the prize while remaining patient, calm, and in the now. Appreciate, too, those people who are around you now; try to make time for friends who don't immediately fit into your future plans.

REVERSED MEANING

When reversed, the Three of Wands shows communication problems. Plans are delayed and it may be difficult to make progress in your projects. Relationships can suffer under this influence, as you find it hard to express yourself and understand what others are saying. Misunderstandings may make you feel needlessly isolated. If this applies to you, resist the frustration that this influence brings and go with a slower pace for a while. Overall, however, these are minor negatives; this is still a card of good fortune, even when reversed, so don't let glitches become a distraction. You can still succeed.

FOUR OF WANDS

KEY MEANINGS: Freedom, creativity, and domestic happiness

UPRIGHT MEANING

This lovely card reveals success after completion—a time for reward. Socially, you will have the opportunity to celebrate and really enjoy yourself; the card predicts you will be brimming with confidence and full of vitality. You also establish yourself in your work and at home, completing a building or remodeling project or moving to a larger property. The vibe of the card is putting down roots, just like the wands. People around you note your willingness to be a pillar of the community and involve yourself in local issues and social events. In work, your talent is appreciated, and you are full of ideas and enthusiasm. Spiritually, the card shows that you share your light with others.

This often comes up in readings to predict that a new partner or love interest will open their hearts and express love and affection. It is also known as the honeymoon card—literally, or as a time to celebrate, run free, and enjoy what life has to offer. It is auspicious for creativity, and artistic projects flourish under the uplifting influence of the Four of Wands.

REVERSED MEANING

When reversed, this is one of the few minor arcana cards that retains its positive meaning, albeit with minor irritations. You don't get all the time you need to focus on doing what you love—from traveling to creative projects and socializing—and you may experience some disruption to plans. In this position, you might just be feeling invisible and not heard. However, if you are feeling too much like the outsider, consider if your environment is right—it's likely that it's them, not you. Overall, however, this unsettled phase will soon pass as the sunny aspect of the upright card prevails.

FIVE OF WANDS

KEY MEANINGS: Competition and debates

UPRIGHT MEANING

The traditional meaning of this Five of Wands is competition, and the message is to hold your position, rather than compromise. Unlike the Five of Swords, this card does not predict outright battle, but there will be fiery opinions and a lack of agreement, at least for now. Misunderstandings abound, particularly in work matters. You may find yourself in meetings during which everyone is talking at once, defending their position rather than reaching a consensus; it's a fight just to be heard.

Scheduling problems and delays to travel plans are an additional meaning, so double-check travel documents and emails, appointments, accounts, and agendas; pay close attention to any written documents.

The Five of Wands often comes up in readings to show being surrounded by people with strong opinions, particularly in families; in education, it predicts that you will need to compete hard in tests or examinations—but you can succeed. On a lighter note, the card can also show competitions that are important to you, such as sporting events.

REVERSED MEANING

The reversed meaning of the Five is deception and misinformation. You may be misled, so carefully consider the source of messages before you make assumptions; what you hear may be exaggerated or untrue. In its most negative aspect, the card can show dishonesty.

In general, the Five of Wands can show you feeling stressed and in a weak position, and if so, it is better to keep your own counsel just for now, or at least be highly selective about the people you choose to trust. An additional meaning of the card is litigation.

SIX OF WANDS

KEY MEANINGS: Victory

UPRIGHT MEANING

This card signifies deserved success. The Six of Wands is a very welcome card if you have been struggling recently and feeling unsure if your hard work will finally pay off. The card often relates to work, career, and projects and can show promotion and a new contract or bid; it can also reveal that an outstanding legal matter will go in your favor. Enjoy this happy time and don't be afraid to share your accomplishment; others will support and applaud you. It's time to bask in glory, be self-satisfied, and make space to celebrate, regardless of how busy you may be.

In personal relationships, the card shows that feelings are declared—and will be well received. The card can also indicate a proposal when it appears close to emotion cards such as the Ace of Cups, Two of Cups, Ten of Cups, and the major arcana card VI, The Lovers. This explains the additional meaning of the Six of Wands for celebrations, such as weddings or attending parties and degree ceremonies.

A traditional meaning of the card is good news, which can relate to any life aspect—love, property, education and work, and decision-making. Look to the other cards that appear close to the Six of Wands in a reading to determine the nature of the news on the way.

REVERSED MEANING

Unfortunately, when the Six of Wands reverses, the reward you have hoped for doesn't materialize when you need it to. But all is not lost—this is a card of delay rather than cancellation, so hold fast to your goals. The wait for news may be frustrating, but this is due to circumstances beyond your control rather than a reflection on your abilities. The message is to be as patient as you can, and distract yourself with other tasks (rather than check your emails and text messages every five minutes).

The card can also show you being let down by others, which dints your confidence. However, as with all the tarot's minor arcana cards, this is a passing phase, so try not to take such disappointments to heart.

An additional interpretation is pride, which in the reversed position can reveal an arrogant, self-important individual.

SEVEN OF WANDS

KEY MEANINGS: Courage, effort, and challenges

UPRIGHT MEANING

The Seven of Wands reveals obstacles in your path, but you will keep going and overcome them. Success is in reach. The card is particularly relevant to work and career matters and highlights all negotiations; regardless of how difficult the conversation becomes, there's a need to keep talking and stay in conversation until you are satisfied with the outcome. You will need to stand tall, and by being very clear on your position, you can win.

There's a noble aspect, too, about this card, and it often comes up in a reading to show you may be defending others, not just your own interests. In this sense, the Seven of Wands is the card of the advocate, and you may find you need to stand up for those who are not able to speak for themselves. Morality is important to you now, so the Seven of Wands shows you may become the spokesperson for a group—such as a committee or jury. The task isn't an easy one, but you will persist.

In relationships, there are hurdles, and you may need to fight for love. This can be only temporary, however, so by all means stand up for your relationship in the short-term, provided you are sure your partner will return your loyalty.

REVERSED MEANING

When reversed, the Seven of Wands can indicate that you doubt your purpose. You may struggle to be heard and may have to overcome constant obstacles—but now it's unclear if it's all going to be worthwhile. As a result, the card can show anxiety and hesitation. An additional meaning is feeling overwhelmed with continual problems, particularly if this Seven appears with the "burden" card, the Ten of Wands. If so, the message here is to focus on the areas where you can still make a difference, while accepting the things you cannot change. This applies to relationships, too, so ask which imperfections you can live with and which aspects—such as your partner's attitude or circumstances—are nonnegotiable.

EIGHT OF WANDS

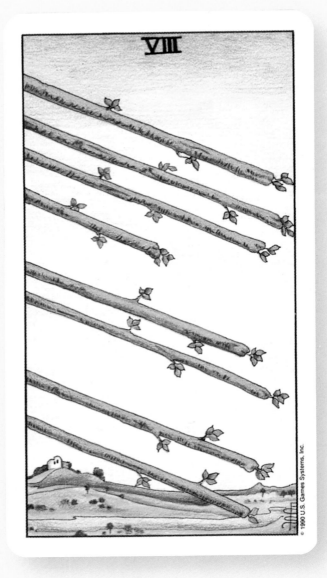

KEY MEANINGS: News and travel

UPRIGHT MEANING

Along with the Ace, the Eight of Wands is one of the most positive cards of the suit. It brings lots of communication, so you may be inundated with emails, calls, and exciting offers. If you have felt held back, or stuck waiting for decisions, you will soon have positive news. All your projects grow wings, moving swiftly forward. Just be prepared for the shift; fast, frantic events will energize you, but you will also need to prioritize any offers.

Don't feel you have to say yes to everything. Choose wisely and enjoy this frenetic, exciting influence.

In relationships, the Eight of Wands can bring great news about love, particularly if you have been separated from a partner recently or are waiting to hear from a potential partner. You may be traveling soon to see one another.

Additionally, the card has often come up in readings to show the professions of carpentry and scaffolding—work that involves using or building a framework.

REVERSED MEANING

When reversed, the simple meaning of the card is delay. You may have lots of pending work to finish and may be waiting for a particular decision that will unblock other ambitions, but just for now, you'll need to be patient. It's also important to be discreet about any grievances you have just now.

In relationships, you may be finding it hard to communicate and as a result be drawn into petty arguments. If you have hopes for a new love, you may be feeling disappointed by the person's lack of contact. Look to the surrounding cards for indictors as to what this means; negative cards such as the Three or Ten of Swords or The Lovers reversed suggest that this potential relationship may not get off the ground. More positive cards, such as the upright Lovers or the Ace, Two, Six, Nine, or Ten of Cups, say that there is still hope you'll connect again.

An additional meaning of the reversed card is jealousy.

NINE OF WANDS

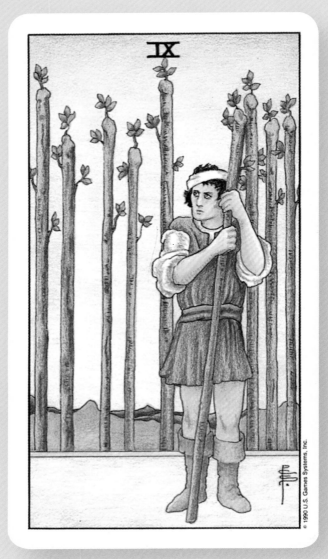

KEY MEANINGS: Defense and strength

UPRIGHT MEANING

The upright Nine of Wands shows that you are in a very strong position. You have fought long and hard to get where you are, and have endured heavy challenges, particularly in work. Being constantly vigilant and ingenious can be exhausting, however, so use your energy wisely; plan all activities meticulously and don't overexert yourself, and you will have all the resources you need to see you through. Thankfully, as with all minor arcana cards, this influence will not last forever. You won't always need to defend yourself to this degree, or make so many sacrifices.

This card also highlights the fine balance between being adequately defended and being defensive. While it's appropriate to establish and protect your boundaries, defensiveness keeps you in a negative mind-set; the Nine often comes up in a reading to show a person who is fearful that his or her idea or other work will be stolen—but this is just a perception rather than reality. It can also show an unwillingness to hand in an assignment or to make your work public in some other way due to fear of rejection or criticism. If so, it's time to let go—you have worked hard, and your efforts will meet with appreciation and support.

REVERSED MEANING

When the Nine of Wands is reversed, you endure strong opposition, which seems unfair. You put in hard work—but receive little thanks in return. You give your all, but it still doesn't seem to be enough, so you may be at the mercy of an unreasonable boss or demanding children, friends, or clients. This situation is demotivating, so you become fixed on getting through tasks without enjoying the aspects of your work that used to be satisfying. Equally, you could be the one who is obstinate and inflexible in your attitude.

The reversed card can also show issues with boundaries. Someone may be invading your territory. In relationships, you may be dealing with an individual who is acting defensively because you are veering into uncomfortable territory for them.

TEN OF WANDS

KEY MEANINGS: Responsibilities and a burden

UPRIGHT MEANING

The upright Ten of Wands reveals that you are carrying too much on your shoulders just now. You may have become so used to being overloaded that you've lost sight of the reason you're doing the work. It's a common card for homemakers and entrepreneurs, those of you who must multitask and constantly respond to a wide range of demands. Consider saying no to any future requests and decide which projects or jobs you can stop or hand over to someone else. There's a real need here for delegation and support from others. No one expects you to carry this on your own, and this goes for emotional burdens, too—they need to be shared. The card can also suggest that you may be carrying issues from the past. On a more positive note, the card reveals that you can be successful, albeit with careful management of time and resources.

This card can show up in a reading to reveal that you may need to look for less demanding work, but you feel too drained by your present job to spend time searching. This puts you in a catch-22: The situation can't change until you pull back from current responsibilities and invest what energy you possess into changing your circumstances. The Ten of Wands can also show that relationships are neglected because all your attention is on work.

Also note that if the Ten of Wands comes up as the you/situation card in a reading, you or the person you are reading for may not be receptive to the reading simply because too much is going on. Lay the cards again or wait three days.

REVERSED MEANING

When reversed, the card's meaning is very similar to that of the upright card, except that some of the burdens may be more perceived than real. This may be a sign of ongoing stress, where every task gets framed as a potential problem. The message here is to try to lighten up a little and take some of the pressure off yourself—you don't need to be perfect. Obstinacy is one of the card's meanings, so do ask yourself if you have created too much self-pressure, fixating on impossible goals.

The reversed card can also show you being caught in an exhausting grind between work and domestic commitments because you are trying to keep everyone happy. Make a vow to make some space for your own needs—you need to please yourself, too. When you can do this, you'll see the way ahead more clearly.

PAGE OF WANDS

KEY MEANINGS: Good news and communication

UPRIGHT MEANING

AS A PERSON: A talkative, entertaining individual, the Page of Wands often turns up in reading to denote a writer. His wand is his pen, his way to express himself in the world at large. Equally, he may be a marketing executive, salesperson, actor, or team manager—any role that relies on personality and great communication skills. This Page is a hard worker, dedicated and enthusiastic, and charming company. He can influence others—just be aware that he can get bored easily and move on to whatever attracts him next (so if you see him as a potential lover, note his actions as well as his words). An additional interpretation of the Page is a reunion with a friend or old colleague with whom you will enjoy chatting and reminiscing.

AS THE "YOU" CARD IN A READING: Express yourself.

AS AN INFLUENCE: The Page of Wands in a reading brings good news about projects and situations that require negotiation. Messages, urgent emails, and phone calls may be demanding, but cool the fire and take a measured view before you react. Assess just how much work you need to do. The atmosphere overall, however, is one of trust, and you can rely upon information you receive. Pages suggest young or new situations, from relationships to work.

The Page of Wands can bring a creative enterprise or job offer—and, while the status of the job may not be as high as you might expect, the overall package may appeal, at least in theory. Do, however, check the details and practicalities before you agree to anything.

See page 83 for meanings if two or more Pages fall close together in a reading.

REVERSED MEANING

When reversed, the Page of Wands brings delays. Messages go astray and communication gets complicated. The Page reversed talks much like his upright counterpart, but the theme of the conversation is negative and rather relentless. As the upright Page holds fast to his goals, so the reversed Page won't let a morose subject drop. The card can also show stubbornness and an inability to listen to others' opinions.

This Page is fickle and does not follow through what he initiates. Eventually, his enthusiasm or obsessions burn out, he becomes easily bored or distracted, and he leaves you to deal with any fallout.

An additional meaning is problems with literacy and can apply to a child or young person struggling with written communication or speech.

KNIGHT OF WANDS

KEY MEANINGS: Speed and action

UPRIGHT MEANING

AS A PERSON: Creative and dynamic, the Knight of Wands is an innovator and likes to do things his way. He inspires those around him and is excellent at networking to promote his ideas. He may be a traveler or visitor, and he will have had many experiences and stories to tell. He is, however, impatient to get things done and can make snap judgments about people based on first impressions. As a potential partner, he can show a charismatic, talkative individual who may take things a little too fast at first.

AS THE "YOU" CARD IN A READING: Fire up your ambition.

AS AN INFLUENCE: Events speed up. Any blocks to progress will be lifted, so this is a welcome card if you have been waiting for decisions or have generally been feeling stuck. You can now have the conversations and action you need to move your projects on; follow your intuition and push forward. This card is particularly auspicious for moving house, finding new work, and making progress on personal and professional projects.

In readings, this Knight often appears to predict a successful writing project. In other creative pursuits, you attract acknowledgment and support, both emotionally and financially.

An additional meaning of the card is travel and emigration.

See page 85 for meanings if two or more Knights fall close together in a reading.

REVERSED MEANING

In general, the reversed Knight of Wands reveals a creative block or miscommunication—so emails go astray and other messages are not delivered. The reversed Knight also indicates delays and deferred decisions; you may feel frustrated at the lack of progress. Know that this influence is temporary and will pass. In the meantime, hold fast to your plans and your self-belief.

As a person, the reversed Knight is egotistical. He thrives on status but is generally unwilling to do any hard work to deserve it; regardless, he will step up to take the credit. Insincere and attention-seeking, he acts out of self-interest.

QUEEN OF WANDS

KEY MEANINGS: Creativity and focus

UPRIGHT MEANING

AS A PERSON: This Queen is often the card of the artisan, entrepreneur, counselor, organizer, or leader—the writer, producer, marketer, or business administrator: whatever relies upon spark and communication for success. Sociable and supportive, she is intensely loyal, just like her associated sign of Aries. This self-aware Queen is also in touch with her intuition, so she makes good choices in relationships. The Queen of Wands often loves nature and animals, too.

AS THE "YOU" CARD IN A READING: Step in to your power.

AS AN INFLUENCE: Ideas flourish, and you can now show others what you can do. This is no time for reticence; fire up your enthusiasm and express yourself. Reflect, also, on how you are managing your life just now, to make sure you have the time to make space for the opportunities coming your way. Overall, though, the Queen of Wands shows you will have the strength you need, and your relationships, too, are energized—romance, friendships, family ties, and professional contacts.

See page 87 for meanings if two or more Queens fall close together in a reading.

REVERSED MEANING

You may feel controlled when the Queen of Wands reverses due to others' pointless interference. There is a great need for organization—but disorder rules. This may be because you, or someone close, has taken on too much and cannot admit it. Consider if this is a pattern—a way of avoiding being who you are, due to fear of rejection.

As a person, the reversed Queen of Wands breaks promises. She can be envious and does not want anyone around her to shine more brightly.

KING OF WANDS

KEY MEANINGS: Abundance, generosity, and creativity

UPRIGHT MEANING

AS A PERSON: This King of Wands is a man of the world, and it's likely that he has traveled widely, experiencing many cultures and countries. Talkative and energetic, his ideal vocations include business and management, communications and marketing, the travel industry, acting, and other roles that depend on self-motivation and individuality. He may be self-employed, running a business or acting as a freelance consultant.

He has wisdom and very high standards that he applies to himself and those around him, and strong integrity. Courteous and considerate, he stays true to his values and acts according to his moral code. He is open and self-aware and does not judge other people on their backgrounds or beliefs; he often learns by listening to people talk about their experiences. As a free spirit, he respects others who don't conform. As a potential partner, he is passionate and communicative.

AS THE "YOU" CARD IN A READING: Be a free spirit.

AS AN INFLUENCE: This is the right time to express your ideas and be the individual you are. Summon your entrepreneurial spirit, make a plan, and what you propose will be well received. The practical support you need will be there, but you need to be the initiator. What you do now reflects your truth. Don't let perfectionism get in the way of your creativity—what you do is more than good enough.

See page 89 for meanings if two or more Kings fall close together in a reading.

REVERSED MEANING

This card reversed indicates a time of restriction when you can't get others to see your point of view. Equally, check that you're not going against your intuition if you feel you're not following the right path—drop the self-pressure and be open to alternative routes.

Bullying, selfish, and opinionated, the reversed King as a person is narrow-minded and obsessive about rules. He can be an overbearing manager or a strict parental figure. He does not want to listen to anyone who doesn't agree with him, and, full of self-interest, he is determined to get his own way.

ACKNOWLEDGMENTS

With thanks to: my agent, Chelsey Fox; my editors, Jill Alexander, Renae Haines, and Leah Jenness; my husband, Michael Young; and special tarot friends Kay Stopforth and Christina Archbold; and in memory of Jonathan Dee, mentor extraordinaire, and the much-missed Marjorie Birchnall.

ABOUT THE AUTHOR

Liz Dean is a tarot teacher and professional tarot reader working with the Rider-Waite deck at Psychic Sisters in Selfridges, London. A former editor with a twenty-five-year career in illustrated book publishing, Liz is the author of seven divination decks and books, including *The Victorian Steampunk Tarot*, *Fairy Tale Fortune Cards*, *44 Ways to Talk to Your Angels*, *The Golden Tarot*, *The Mystery of the Tarot*, *The Love Tarot*, and the 300,000-copy bestseller *The Art of Tarot*. Liz was recently featured in *Tarot Masters*, a collection of thirty-eight essays by workshop leaders and speakers from the UK Tarot Conference.

Liz is also an Angelic Reiki Master Teacher and a former coeditor of the UK's leading spiritual magazine, *Kindred Spirit*. She lives in London and Leicestershire, England. You can visit her at www.lizdean.com.

INDEX

Julia Donaldson • A

Petit
Gruffalo

GALLIMARD JEUNESSE

Le Gruffalo disait qu'il n'est jamais très bon
Qu'un Gruffalo se montre dans le grand bois profond.
– Pourquoi? Pourquoi? « *Parce que si tu y vas,*
La Grande Méchante Souris te poursuivra.
Je l'ai connue un jour, dit Gruffalo papa,
Il y a très longtemps de cela. »

– Comment est-elle, papa? C'est ce que je me
demande.
Terriblement méchante et terriblement grande?

– Je ne me souviens pas bien, dit papa Gruffalo.
Il se gratta la tête tout en cherchant ses mots.

Elle a une force terrible
et sa queue bien visible
Est couverte d'écailles
et d'une longueur terrible.

Ses terribles yeux rouges brillent
comme des éclairs,
Ses terribles moustaches sont
comme des fils de fer.

Un soir où il neigeait,
le Gruffalo ronflait.
L'enfant du Gruffalo
dans son coin s'ennuyait.

L'enfant du Gruffalo
n'avait pas peur du tout,
Elle quitta la caverne
à petits pas de loup.
La neige tombait drue,
le vent soufflait sans fin,
Quand l'enfant Gruffalo
partit sur le chemin.

– Ah, ah ! Oh ! Une trace sur le sol enneigé !
Qui est passé par là ? Où va-t-elle me mener ?
Une queue bien visible sortait d'une pile de bois,
La Grande Méchante Souris serait-elle cachée là ?

L'animal apparut. Ses yeux n'étaient pas gros,
Et il n'avait pas de moustache sur son museau.

– Tu n'es pas la souris. « *Oh non, ce n'est pas moi,*
Elle mange là-bas un Gruffalo au chocolat. »

La neige tombait drue, le vent soufflait sans fin,
L'enfant du Gruffalo disait : « Je n'ai peur de rien. »

– Ah, ah ! Oh ! Des marques sur le sol enneigé !
Qui est passé par là ? Où vont-elles me mener ?
Dans un arbre, deux yeux étincelaient dans la nuit,
Seraient-ce les yeux de la Grande Méchante Souris ?

L'animal descendit. Il n'avait pas de queue
Et aucune moustache, pas même un petit peu.

– Tu n'es pas la souris. « *Hou, hou, ce n'est pas moi,*
Elle est là-bas et mange un Gruffalo aux noix. »

La neige tombait drue, le vent soufflait sans fin,
L'enfant du Gruffalo disait : « Je n'ai peur de rien. »

– Ah, ah ! Oh ! Une piste sur le sol enneigé !
Qui est passé par là ? Où va-t-elle me mener ?
Ah, des grosses moustaches et une maison sous terre !
La Grande Méchante Souris est-elle dans son repaire ?

Une créature sortit. Dans ses yeux, pas d'éclairs.
Pas d'écailles sur sa queue, pas de moustaches en fer.

– Tu n'es pas la souris. « *Oh non, ce n'est pas moi,*
Elle boit un thé au Gruffalo au fond du bois. »

L'enfant Gruffalo dit : « C'est une plaisanterie.
Je ne crois plus à la Grande Méchante Souris... »
Elle s'assit sur une souche dans la forêt obscure...

Et aperçut soudain la petite créature.
Pas grande ni méchante,
mais c'était une souris.
– Ça va être très bon
pour mon repas de minuit.

– Avant que tu ne manges, dit alors la souris,
Il faut que tu rencontres une de mes amies.
Elle est grande et méchante et va vite arriver
Quand je lui ferai signe du haut de ce noisetier.

L'enfant du Gruffalo la lâcha sur-le-champ.
– La Grande Méchante Souris ? Elle existe vraiment ?
Dans l'arbre, la souris fit un signe et lui dit :
– La voilà qui s'approche, je ne t'ai pas menti.

La lune se leva comme un disque brillant,
Et une ombre terrible tomba sur le sol blanc.

Quelle est cette bête si grande,
qui paraît si méchante ?
Une queue, des moustaches
d'une longueur terrifiante.
Ses oreilles sont énormes
et elle porte facilement
Une noisette aussi grosse
qu'un rocher géant.

– La Grande Méchante Souris! Oh, moi, je file d'ici!
La souris descendit de son arbre et... sourit.

– Ah, ah ! Oh ! Des empreintes sur le sol enneigé.
Qui est passé par là ? Où vont-elles me mener ?

Elle découvrit le Gruffalo dans sa tanière,

L'enfant du Gruffalo était un peu moins fière.

Elle ne pensait plus du tout qu'elle s'ennuyait...